I0186188

The Beginner's Guide to Sewing: Building Skills One Stitch at a Time

PUBLISHED BY Rebecca Thompson

© **Copyright 2025 - All rights reserved.**

All introductions, analyses, and commentaries contained within this book may not be reproduced, duplicated, or transmitted without direct written permission from the author or the publisher. Under no circumstances will any blame or legal responsibility be held against the publisher or author for any damages, reparation, or monetary loss due to the information contained within this book, either directly or indirectly.

Legal Notice:

This book is only for personal use. You cannot amend, distribute, sell, use, quote, or paraphrase any part of the introductions, analyses, or commentaries within this book, without the consent of the author or publisher.

Disclaimer Notice:

Please note the information contained within this document is for educational and entertainment purposes only. All efforts have been executed to present accurate, up-to-date, reliable, complete information. No warranties of any kind are declared or implied. Readers acknowledge that the author is not engaged in the rendering of legal, financial, medical, or professional advice. The content within this book has been derived from various sources. Please consult a licensed professional before attempting any techniques outlined in this book.

By reading this document, the reader agrees that under no circumstances is the author responsible for any losses, direct or indirect, that are incurred as a result of the use of the information contained within this document, including, but not limited to, errors, omissions, or inaccuracies.

Table of contents

Introduction..4

Chapter 1: The Psychology of Learning to Sew...............9

Chapter 2: Fabric Intelligence — Beyond Cotton and Polyester. 21

Chapter 3: The Strategic Sewing Space 33

Chapter 4: Essential Tools and Equipment Mastery.................... 43

Chapter 5: Pattern Reading as a Second Language 54

Chapter 6: The Foundation — Mastering Seams and Seam Finishes.. 65

Chapter 7: Closures — Beyond Basic Buttons and Zippers......... 75

Chapter 8: Shaping Techniques — Creating Three-Dimensional Form 84

Chapter 9: Advanced Construction Techniques........................... 93

Chapter 10: Specialty Fabrics and Advanced Techniques........... 106

Conclusion — Your Continuing Sewing Journey 116

Introduction

Welcome to the transformative world of sewing, a craft that has accompanied humanity for thousands of years and continues to reinvent itself in every generation. Whether it is the ancient hand-stitching of our ancestors, the careful patchwork quilts passed down in families, or the sleek garments displayed on modern runways, sewing has always been a bridge between creativity, practicality, and personal expression. It is both art and utility, function and beauty, an intersection where imagination takes physical form through fabric and thread.

For many beginners, the first encounter with sewing feels like stepping into a workshop filled with endless possibilities. The tools themselves carry a kind of quiet magic: spools of thread in every imaginable shade, the soft weight of fabric that begs to be transformed, and the simple needle—a small object with immense power to shape and repair. Even the hum of a sewing machine, once unfamiliar, becomes a rhythm that inspires confidence and focus. Sewing is not simply about joining pieces of fabric; it is about piecing together parts of yourself—your patience, your taste, your skill, and your story.

In today's world, where ready-to-wear clothing is available at the tap of a button, one might wonder: why sew at all? The answer lies in the unique satisfaction that sewing provides. When you create something with your own hands, you move beyond the role of consumer and step into the role of maker. You reclaim control over design, quality, and individuality. A garment stitched by you will never be identical to one found on a store rack; it carries the imprint of your choices, your craftsmanship, and your time. It can be as humble as a repaired shirt that continues to serve its purpose or as ambitious as a dress tailored for a milestone event. Each piece you make is infused with meaning, making sewing not only a skill but also a deeply personal practice.

This book was written with beginners in mind—those who may be threading a needle for the very first time or standing in front of a sewing machine with equal parts curiosity and hesitation. Perhaps you've long admired the creativity of others and wondered if you could do the same. Perhaps you've grown frustrated with ill-fitting clothes and want to learn how to make adjustments that reflect your body and comfort. Or maybe you've been drawn to the timeless appeal of handmade items: quilts, bags, costumes, or home décor. Whatever brought you here, know that you are taking the first step into a craft that will reward you in ways far beyond what you might expect.

The beauty of sewing is that it meets you where you are. You can begin with something as small as fixing a loose button or hemming a pair of pants, and from there, the possibilities expand. Sewing is a skill that grows with you. The more you practice, the more you unlock, moving from simple stitches to complex patterns, from alterations to original designs. And unlike many hobbies that demand expensive tools or specialized spaces, sewing can be adapted to your circumstances. A small corner table can serve as your workshop, and with just a few essential tools, you can embark on projects that carry lasting value.

Beyond practicality, sewing connects you to a greater tradition. Across cultures and eras, sewing has been a way of preserving stories and heritage. Think of the embroidery passed from one generation to the next, carrying motifs unique to a region or family. Think of wartime, when sewing meant mending uniforms or making do with limited resources. Even in today's sustainability movement, sewing has re-emerged as a solution to wastefulness, encouraging people to repair, repurpose, and recycle clothing rather than discard it. By learning to sew, you join a lineage of makers who understood that fabric is more than material—it is memory, resource, and possibility.

At its heart, this book is about empowerment. Sewing is not just a technical skill; it is a practice that nurtures patience, focus, and creativity. It teaches you to problem-solve when seams don't align, to experiment when fabric resists, and to celebrate small victories along the way. The process is as rewarding as the finished product. Even mistakes, which every beginner will encounter, become part of your journey. A crooked seam today can be unpicked and corrected tomorrow, and in the process, you learn resilience. In a fast-paced world where many experiences are fleeting, sewing offers something rare: the chance to slow down, to engage deeply with your hands and mind, and to create something lasting.

This guide will take you on a structured journey, beginning with the very basics—understanding fabrics, learning how to thread a needle, practicing fundamental stitches—and gradually moving into more complex techniques. You will learn how to read patterns, how to measure and cut accurately, and how to troubleshoot common issues. Along the way, you will also discover the joy of personalization: choosing fabrics that speak to you, adding details that reflect your personality, and eventually crafting garments or items that are uniquely yours.

Yet this book is not only about skill-building; it is also about cultivating a mindset. As a beginner, you may feel overwhelmed by the technical language or intimidated by the flawless work of experienced sewists. But remember: every expert once sat where you are now, fumbling with thread or wondering how to keep a seam straight. Progress in sewing, as in any craft, comes step by step, stitch by stitch. Patience and practice are your greatest tools. This book aims to be both a teacher and a companion, offering encouragement and clarity as you develop your abilities.

Sewing also invites you to explore your individuality. In a culture where so many items are mass-produced, handmade work stands out as a declaration of uniqueness. Your projects can be bold or subtle, traditional or experimental. Some people find joy in tailoring clothing that fits perfectly, while others prefer the freedom of quilting abstract designs or experimenting with costumes. Whatever direction you take, sewing is an open invitation to express yourself. Your finished pieces are not just fabric held together by thread; they are reflections of your imagination, shaped into reality by your hands.

In addition to self-expression, sewing opens doors to community. Around the world, sewing circles, online forums, and workshops bring people together to share techniques, trade patterns, and encourage one another. Learning in community accelerates growth and deepens enjoyment. You will find that many sewists are eager to pass on their knowledge, knowing that the craft flourishes through shared experience. Even if you practice alone at home, you are never truly isolated; you are part of a global network of makers, each contributing to a collective tapestry of creativity.

This introduction is an invitation: to embrace the craft with curiosity, to allow yourself the freedom to learn, and to trust in the process. You may begin with a single project, but with time, sewing will weave itself into your life in ways you might not anticipate. It may become a meditative practice that calms your mind after a busy day. It may turn into a practical skill that saves you money and reduces waste. It may even blossom into a passion that connects you to others or evolves into a career. However it takes root, sewing has the power to transform—not only the fabrics you work with, but also the way you see yourself as a creator.

As you turn these pages and begin your journey, remember that sewing is not a race. There is no deadline, no competition, only your personal rhythm. Take joy in the small steps, whether it is threading a machine for the first time, sewing a seam that holds firm, or wearing something you made with pride. Each moment is a stitch in your growth as a maker. And just as a single stitch is small yet essential to the whole, your early efforts—no matter how imperfect—are the foundation of everything that follows.

So, welcome. Welcome to a world where fabric becomes story, where thread becomes expression, and where you, needle in hand, become part of a timeless tradition. Welcome to sewing.

Chapter 1: The Psychology of Learning to Sew

"Every expert was once a beginner. Every pro was once an amateur. Every icon was once an unknown." — Robin Sharma

1.1 Understanding Your Learning Style in Sewing

The first step to mastering sewing isn't about needles, fabric, or even patterns—it's about understanding yourself. Every individual absorbs, processes, and retains information differently, and recognizing your personal learning style can be the difference between frustration and fulfillment on your sewing journey. Too often, beginners give up not because the craft is beyond their reach, but because they are trying to learn in a way that doesn't align with how their brain naturally works. Sewing, like any skill, rewards patience and adaptability, but those qualities flourish best when paired with strategies tailored to your preferred way of learning.

Most people lean into one or more of three primary learning styles: **visual**, **kinesthetic**, and **auditory**. None of these is inherently superior; they are simply different pathways to acquiring and strengthening skills. Some people thrive when they see instructions mapped out clearly. Others need to feel fabric in their hands and experiment physically. Still others learn most effectively when they hear explanations spoken aloud or engage in conversation. In practice, many learners benefit from a blend of all three, but identifying your dominant style allows you to prioritize the resources and methods that resonate most with you. Sewing is an art and a science, and approaching it with this self-awareness sets you up for steady, enjoyable progress.

Visual Learning Techniques

Visual learners find clarity when information is presented in images, diagrams, or step-by-step demonstrations. For someone who learns visually, sewing patterns are not just blueprints—they are lifelines. The symbols, lines, and illustrations provide a roadmap that transforms a flat piece of fabric into a three-dimensional garment. If you fall into this category, you may find yourself naturally drawn to instruction books with clear pictures, sewing blogs that feature detailed photographs, or video tutorials that show each step in real time.

One effective strategy for visual learners is the use of **pattern diagrams**. When you first look at a pattern, it might appear overwhelming: strange symbols, dotted lines, arrows, and unfamiliar terminology. But once you begin to decode the visual language, it becomes intuitive. Highlighting or color-coding these diagrams can enhance your comprehension. For instance, marking seam lines in one color and cutting lines in another can make the steps clearer, reducing the chance of mistakes. This technique is particularly helpful for beginners who may still be unfamiliar with sewing vocabulary.

Instructional videos are another invaluable tool. Platforms like YouTube or dedicated sewing websites offer thousands of tutorials on everything from threading a machine to mastering a French seam. The advantage of video is that you can pause, rewind, and replay until the motion becomes familiar. For a visual learner, this is like having a teacher on demand, showing you not only what to do but how it should look at every stage. Watching a hem being pinned or a dart being stitched gives you a reference point to compare your own work against.

Additionally, **color-coding systems** can turn complex projects into digestible steps. Imagine working on a quilt where each piece of fabric must be arranged precisely. Assigning a different color marker to each section of the design helps maintain order and ensures consistency. Visual learners often thrive when they can transform abstract directions into concrete images, and color is one of the simplest yet most powerful ways to achieve this.

As a visual learner, your strength lies in your ability to see the "big picture." You may excel at imagining how a garment will look before it's finished, or at spotting subtle differences in fabric drape or hue. Use this ability to your advantage. Create mood boards of designs that inspire you. Sketch rough drafts of projects. Surround yourself with imagery that fuels your creativity, and you'll find the technical aspects of sewing come more naturally when supported by a strong visual foundation.

Kinesthetic Approach Benefits

For kinesthetic learners, the key to understanding sewing lies not in seeing or hearing instructions, but in doing. If you are a kinesthetic learner, your body remembers what your eyes or ears might not fully register. You learn by touching, by experimenting, by making mistakes with your hands until the motion becomes second nature. In sewing, this approach is not only valid but often essential. No matter how many diagrams you study or videos you watch, there is no substitute for the feeling of fabric moving under your fingertips or the rhythm of guiding cloth through a machine.

One of the most powerful tools for kinesthetic learners is **hands-on practice with different fabric textures and weights**. Cotton behaves differently from silk, and denim requires a different touch than chiffon. By physically working with these materials, you develop what's called **muscle memory**. Your fingers learn the resistance of heavy fabrics, the slipperiness of lightweight ones, and the exact pressure needed to maintain even stitches. Over time, this embodied knowledge becomes second nature, enabling you to adjust instinctively.

Exercises that emphasize repetition are especially beneficial. For example, sewing a series of straight lines on scrap fabric, even without a specific project in mind, trains your body to guide the material smoothly. Each pass strengthens your precision, and soon you'll notice that your stitches grow straighter and more consistent without conscious effort. Similarly, practicing curves, corners, and backstitches repeatedly builds confidence, so when you encounter these techniques in an actual project, they feel familiar rather than intimidating.

Kinesthetic learners also benefit from **trial and error**. While visual learners might avoid mistakes by carefully studying instructions beforehand, kinesthetic learners often discover the best solutions by experimenting. Don't be discouraged if your first seam puckers or your first buttonhole looks uneven. The act of correcting mistakes teaches you as much as, if not more than, following instructions perfectly. With every misstep, your hands learn what to adjust: how to reduce tension, how to handle fabric gently, how to realign pieces with accuracy.

Another strategy is to engage in **tactile exercises** outside of formal projects. Handling swatches of different fabrics, folding and unfolding them, stretching them in various directions—all of these actions expand your tactile vocabulary. When you later choose materials for a garment, you'll rely on more than sight; you'll know from touch how the fabric will drape, move, and respond under a needle. For a kinesthetic learner, this sensory familiarity transforms uncertainty into confidence.

The kinesthetic approach also aligns with the meditative, grounding qualities of sewing. There is something profoundly satisfying about using your hands to create tangible results. The process itself can reduce stress, sharpen focus, and offer a sense of accomplishment that goes beyond the finished garment. In other words, for kinesthetic learners, the act of sewing is as rewarding as the outcome.

Auditory Processing Methods

Auditory learners absorb knowledge most effectively when they hear it spoken or when they engage in conversation. For someone with this style, sewing can initially seem more challenging because the craft is so visual and tactile. Yet there are abundant ways to adapt auditory strategies to this skill, and when done intentionally, they can be just as effective.

One of the simplest methods is listening to **sewing podcasts**. Many experienced sewists host shows where they discuss techniques, troubleshoot common problems, or share stories about their projects. Hearing others talk through the steps or challenges can spark insights that stick in your mind. Unlike reading an instruction manual, which might feel flat, listening engages your imagination. You begin to picture what the speaker describes, creating a vivid mental map of the process.

Guided tutorials are another invaluable resource. While visual learners rely on the imagery of videos, auditory learners focus on the spoken instructions. Listening closely to how a teacher describes pinning fabric or adjusting machine tension can clarify steps in ways that static diagrams cannot. You may find it useful to follow along by sewing in real time while listening, treating the tutorial as if the instructor were right beside you.

Auditory learning also thrives in **social settings**. Sewing circles, whether in-person or online, provide opportunities to exchange ideas verbally. Explaining a process to someone else, or hearing them explain it to you, reinforces understanding. The casual discussions in these communities often include tips and tricks not found in books—those small details that make a big difference in practice. By asking questions, listening to others' experiences, and sharing your own, you anchor knowledge in conversation rather than isolation.

Even reading instructions aloud to yourself can be surprisingly effective. By vocalizing each step, you engage your auditory memory, making it easier to recall later. Some learners also create simple rhymes or verbal cues to remember key concepts. For instance, repeating "right sides together" aloud as you pin fabric can help prevent the common mistake of sewing pieces with the wrong sides facing.

Finally, auditory learners often find music or rhythm useful in enhancing concentration. The steady beat of background music, or even the natural rhythm of a sewing machine, can serve as a kind of metronome, keeping you engaged and focused. By leaning into sound, you transform sewing into a multisensory experience that supports your natural strengths.

Bringing It Together

Understanding your learning style is not about limiting yourself but about unlocking doors. You may discover that you are primarily visual but gain surprising insights when you experiment kinesthetically. Or you may be an auditory learner who benefits from pairing spoken instructions with diagrams. The point is not to box yourself into a single category but to recognize the methods that resonate most strongly with you and use them as a foundation. From there, you can expand, combining approaches to deepen your mastery.

Sewing is a craft rich in variety, and its learning pathways reflect that diversity. Whether you learn best by seeing, doing, or hearing, there is space for you in this world of fabric and thread. By honoring your unique learning style, you make the process more enjoyable, reduce frustration, and accelerate your growth.

Remember: the stitches you make are not only on fabric—they are in your mind, your memory, and your confidence as a maker.

1.2 Overcoming Common Mental Barriers

The practical challenges of sewing—threading needles, deciphering patterns, managing fabric—are tangible and straightforward compared to the mental hurdles that many beginners encounter. While hands can be trained with time and practice, the mind often resists with self-doubt, frustration, or unrealistic expectations. These mental barriers can be more limiting than any technical skill gap. Recognizing them and addressing them head-on is a vital part of learning to sew.

One of the most persistent challenges is perfectionism. Many beginners approach their first projects with an unspoken belief that success means flawless execution. They imagine crisp seams, even stitches, and garments indistinguishable from professional work. The reality, however, is that learning to sew is a messy process. Crooked hems, uneven tension, and mismatched seams are not failures but milestones. They are evidence that you are engaging with the craft. To embrace the value of imperfection requires a shift in mindset. Instead of seeing mistakes as proof of inadequacy, reframe them as essential teachers. That slightly puckered seam is not the end of the road but a direct invitation to adjust your technique and try again. Every experienced sewist carries a history of errors that formed the foundation of their mastery. The sooner you allow yourself the freedom to be "perfectly imperfect," the sooner you open the door to progress.

Another common obstacle is intimidation. Sewing can appear overwhelming when confronted with the complexity of a finished garment. Looking at a tailored jacket or a pleated dress can create a sense of impossibility, especially when your own projects are still at the stage of simple tote bags or pillow covers. The way to disarm this intimidation is to break down large projects into manageable components. A jacket is not a single insurmountable task; it is a collection of smaller techniques—seams, buttonholes, linings—each of which can be practiced independently. By focusing on one element at a time, you transform daunting projects into a series of achievable steps. This progressive approach not only builds technical ability but also instills confidence. Completing smaller challenges gradually conditions you to believe that more complex garments are within your reach.

Closely tied to intimidation is the habit of comparison. Beginners often measure their early work against that of seasoned sewists whose skill is the product of years, sometimes decades, of experience. Social media magnifies this trap, presenting polished images that disguise the mistakes and frustrations that undoubtedly occurred behind the scenes. When you compare your first efforts to the perfected results of others, you rob yourself of the joy of learning. The more constructive path is to develop personal benchmarks for growth. Instead of asking whether your garment looks as professional as something in a store, ask whether your stitches are straighter than they were last month. Notice if you are more comfortable using your sewing machine or if you can now interpret pattern instructions that once seemed cryptic. These self-referenced measures place emphasis on your own progress, which is the only comparison that truly matters. By cultivating awareness of growth rather than focusing on shortcomings, you free yourself to appreciate the journey as much as the destination.

Overcoming these mental barriers is about cultivating resilience and perspective. Sewing, like any worthwhile endeavor, is not a linear path. There will be frustrations, missteps, and moments of doubt. But within these challenges lie the richest opportunities for growth. Each mistake is a stitch in the fabric of your learning, and when viewed as such, they become part of your story rather than an obstacle to it.

1.3 Building a Sustainable Learning Mindset

While overcoming barriers clears the way, sustaining momentum requires a deliberate mindset. Sewing is not a skill mastered overnight; it is cultivated through patience, consistency, and an ongoing commitment to growth. Establishing a sustainable learning mindset ensures that you not only begin your sewing journey with enthusiasm but also carry it forward long enough to experience real transformation.

One of the most effective tools for building this mindset is goal setting. Lofty aspirations like "I want to make all my clothes" or "I want to sew like a professional" can inspire, but they can also overwhelm. What you need instead are goals that balance ambition with practicality. Using a structured framework like SMART—specific, measurable, achievable, relevant, and time-bound—turns vague hopes into actionable plans. Rather than saying "I want to learn to sew dresses," you might commit to "completing one simple shift dress within the next two months, practicing seams and hems along the way." This kind of goal has a clear outcome, a realistic timeframe, and measurable progress markers. Each completed project then becomes both an achievement in itself and a stepping-stone toward larger ambitions.

Another cornerstone of a sustainable mindset is documenting progress. Sewing lends itself beautifully to visual records, and keeping a photo journal of your projects allows you to see just how far you've come. A snapshot of your very first uneven hem alongside later garments with crisp edges tells a story of improvement that is easy to overlook in the moment. Some sewists also keep written reflections, noting challenges faced, techniques learned, or adjustments made to patterns. These records become more than a log; they are a source of encouragement when motivation dips. Looking back on your growth provides tangible evidence that you are evolving, even if the pace sometimes feels slow.

Skill checklists can also play a role in sustaining learning. By listing specific techniques—such as sewing a zipper, making buttonholes, or binding a quilt—you create a map of competencies to work toward. Checking off each skill as you master it is both satisfying and motivating. It transforms sewing from an amorphous craft into a structured journey where each accomplishment propels you forward.

Community is another powerful driver of a sustainable learning mindset. Sewing can be solitary, but it thrives in connection. Local guilds, workshops, and maker spaces offer environments where you can learn alongside others, ask questions, and witness different approaches. Online forums and social media groups provide similar benefits, connecting you with sewists across the globe who share advice, encouragement, and inspiration. Engaging with a community does more than accelerate technical learning; it creates accountability. When you share your projects with others, you naturally commit to continuing. Their feedback, whether through constructive tips or simple words of encouragement, reinforces your sense of progress and belonging.

Equally important is recognizing the ebb and flow of motivation. There will be seasons when sewing excites you and projects come easily, and others when enthusiasm wanes. A sustainable mindset acknowledges these fluctuations without judgment. During low-energy periods, it may be enough to repair a small tear or organize your fabric stash, maintaining a connection to the craft without forcing large projects. When inspiration returns, you'll be ready to dive back in without the weight of guilt or pressure.

Finally, sustainability in sewing involves cultivating patience and joy in the process itself. If the only satisfaction you seek comes from finished garments, you may struggle during the inevitable trial-and-error stages. But if you learn to appreciate the rhythm of stitching, the quiet focus of pressing seams, and the tactile pleasure of fabric, sewing becomes more than a skill—it becomes a practice. Like gardening or cooking, it offers a way of slowing down, engaging your senses, and finding meaning in small, deliberate actions. This mindset transforms sewing from a task to be completed into a lifelong source of fulfillment.

Chapter 2: Fabric Intelligence — Beyond Cotton and Polyester

Did you know that the ancient Egyptians created linen so fine it was transparent, with thread counts exceeding 500 per square inch—rivaling today's luxury fabrics?

2.1 Natural Fiber Deep Dive

Before a needle pierces fabric, before a pattern is cut, before a garment takes shape, every sewing project begins with a decision about material. Fabric is the canvas upon which your creativity unfolds, but it is far from a neutral backdrop. Each fiber carries unique qualities that dictate not only the final look and feel of a garment but also the very experience of sewing it. Understanding natural fibers—their strengths, quirks, and histories—is like learning the personalities of new friends. Some are forgiving, some temperamental, some regal, and some humble. Choosing the right one means aligning your project with the properties of the material so that fabric and design work in harmony rather than conflict.

Natural fibers can be divided into two main families: protein-based and cellulose-based. There are also newer specialty options derived from natural sources but processed with modern technology. Each group brings its own set of characteristics that affect drape, durability, breathability, and ease of handling.

Protein-Based Fibers

Protein fibers come from animals and are composed of keratin or fibroin, the same proteins found in hair, nails, and other biological structures. Their origins give them natural elasticity, resilience, and warmth—qualities that have made them staples for centuries.

Wool is perhaps the most versatile and storied of these fibers. Derived primarily from sheep, wool is prized for its ability to regulate temperature. Unlike many synthetic fabrics that trap heat, wool fibers naturally insulate while also allowing air circulation. This dual ability comes from their crimped structure, which creates tiny pockets of air that retain warmth in cold conditions yet permit breathability in warmer ones. For the sewist, wool offers both opportunities and challenges. It tailors beautifully, holding shape when pressed, which makes it ideal for structured garments like coats and trousers. At the same time, its tendency to shrink when agitated in water requires care in both preparation and maintenance. Wool's natural elasticity also makes it forgiving; seams stretch slightly under stress, reducing strain on stitches. For beginners, lightweight wools such as gabardine or flannel provide manageable introductions before moving on to finer varieties.

Silk, in contrast, is the queen of luster and strength. Produced by silkworms spinning cocoons of fibroin, silk threads are incredibly strong for their size, rivaling even steel in tensile strength. Yet silk is delicate in other ways, prone to water spotting and abrasion. Its unique combination of strength and fragility requires respect. The reward, however, is unmatched elegance: a drape that flows with gravity, a sheen that catches light like liquid, and a smoothness that flatters the skin. Sewing with silk demands patience and sharp tools, as the slippery surface tends to shift under the presser foot. Tissues or stabilizers can be used to tame its movement, and fine needles help avoid snags. Despite the learning curve, silk offers an education in precision; it forces the sewist to slow down and cultivate control.

Among the luxury animal fibers, **alpaca and cashmere** deserve mention. Alpaca, from the South American camelid, produces fibers that are hollow, making them warmer and lighter than sheep's wool. They lack the lanolin found in sheep's wool, which gives them a hypoallergenic quality. Alpaca resists pilling and felting, making it durable for everyday wear, yet it carries a soft hand that feels luxurious. **Cashmere**, sourced from the undercoat of goats in colder climates, is revered for its extreme softness. Its fibers are fine and delicate, yielding garments with remarkable warmth-to-weight ratios. However, cashmere's delicacy means it stretches more easily under tension and may lose shape without proper structuring. For the sewist, working with these fibers is a lesson in balance—recognizing their exquisite qualities while accommodating their sensitivities through careful construction and finishing techniques.

Cellulose Fiber Characteristics

Where protein fibers come from animals, cellulose fibers are plant-based. They are composed primarily of cellulose, a carbohydrate polymer that forms plant cell walls. These fibers tend to be breathable, absorbent, and durable, making them staples for both ancient and modern wardrobes.

Linen, derived from the stalks of the flax plant, is one of the oldest textiles in human history. The linen cloth of ancient Egypt was prized for its purity, coolness, and ability to withstand time, with some pieces preserved for millennia in tombs. Linen is renowned for its durability; its fibers are stronger than cotton and become softer with each wash. It also excels at moisture absorption, making it a superb fabric for warm climates. The drawback for sewists is its tendency to wrinkle easily, a quality intrinsic to its stiff fiber structure. Sewing with linen, however, is a rewarding experience. Its crisp hand makes it easy to cut and handle, seams press sharply, and the fabric rarely shifts or slips during construction. Beginners often find linen forgiving, and its natural texture adds charm even when wrinkles inevitably appear.

Cotton, perhaps the most ubiquitous of plant fibers, owes its versatility to its ability to adapt to countless weaves and finishes. From the dense twill of denim to the delicate weave of voile, cotton spans an extraordinary range of applications. Its softness and absorbency make it comfortable for everyday wear, while its ease of dyeing allows for vibrant colors and patterns. For the sewist, cotton is a faithful ally. It cuts cleanly, holds shape without excessive slippage, and tolerates pressing and washing well. This combination of qualities makes it the quintessential beginner's fabric. Yet within cotton lies endless variety; working with denim teaches lessons in handling thickness, while lightweight lawn fabric introduces the challenge of delicacy. Thus, cotton is not only versatile for garments but also versatile as a training ground for skill development.

Hemp, long overshadowed by cotton, has experienced a renaissance due to its environmental advantages. Hemp plants grow quickly, require minimal pesticides, and improve soil health, making them one of the most sustainable textile crops. The fibers themselves are strong, durable, and resistant to pests. Hemp fabric shares similarities with linen in texture and durability but often feels rougher in its untreated state. With wear and washing, however, hemp softens significantly while retaining its resilience. Sewing with hemp introduces the sewist to a fabric that bridges tradition and modern sustainability. It teaches patience in handling a fabric that initially resists softness, but the reward is garments that last decades and carry an ethical dimension in their reduced ecological footprint.

Specialty Natural Options

The modern textile world has also expanded the definition of "natural" fibers by developing materials derived from renewable sources but processed with advanced techniques. These fabrics offer intriguing combinations of traditional qualities and innovative improvements.

Bamboo fabric, created from cellulose extracted from bamboo plants, has gained popularity for its moisture-wicking properties and silky hand. It feels soft against the skin, often compared to cashmere or silk, yet retains durability similar to cotton. Bamboo's natural antibacterial properties also make it attractive for garments worn close to the body. For the sewist, bamboo jersey in particular introduces stretch fabrics in a manageable way, combining comfort with elegance.

Modal, made from beech tree cellulose, is another specialty fiber known for its luxurious drape and softness. It resists shrinkage, holds dye well, and offers a smooth texture that elevates everyday garments. Working with modal requires attention because its fluid drape can challenge cutting and sewing precision, but its cooperative nature in sewing—less slippery than silk, more forgiving than rayon—makes it a rewarding choice.

Tencel, or lyocell, represents one of the most eco-conscious developments in modern textiles. Produced from wood pulp, often eucalyptus, in a closed-loop process that recycles solvents, Tencel combines sustainability with exceptional fabric qualities. It drapes like silk, feels cool and smooth on the skin, and has excellent moisture absorption. For the sewist, Tencel presents a middle ground between natural elegance and modern performance. It cuts and sews more easily than silk but still provides garments with a refined, flowing appearance.

These specialty fibers embody the evolving relationship between tradition and innovation in textiles. They remind sewists that fabric knowledge is not static; it continues to expand with advances in science and sustainability.

2.2 Synthetic Fabric Mastery

While natural fibers have millennia of tradition behind them, the twentieth century ushered in a revolution with the invention of synthetic fabrics. These materials, engineered in laboratories rather than harvested from plants or animals, expanded the possibilities of what cloth could do. They offered durability, elasticity, moisture resistance, and other qualities that natural fibers alone could not provide. For sewists, mastering synthetic fabrics is not only about learning how to handle them at the machine but also about understanding when they outperform their natural counterparts and how they can be blended to achieve remarkable results.

Performance is one of the defining features of synthetic textiles. Polyester, for example, has become ubiquitous in activewear because of its ability to wick moisture away from the body and dry quickly. Unlike cotton, which absorbs water and becomes heavy, polyester maintains its lightness and resilience even during strenuous activity. For a sewist, this means polyester garments can be designed for comfort in motion, whether that be running shorts, hiking shirts, or everyday athleisure. Yet polyester can sometimes feel less breathable, so pairing it with mesh panels or designing looser fits can compensate for this drawback.

Spandex, also known as elastane or Lycra, introduced an entirely new dimension of stretch. With the ability to extend several times its length and snap back into shape, spandex transformed not only sportswear but also swimwear, underwear, and fitted garments. Its true strength lies not in being used alone but in blends. A cotton fabric with two to five percent spandex gains flexibility and recovery without sacrificing breathability. Four-way stretch blends—fabrics that stretch both lengthwise and crosswise—are particularly prized for activities that require a wide range of movement, such as yoga or dance. Sewing with these fabrics requires care, as seams must accommodate stretch without breaking. Using stretch stitches, ballpoint needles, and specialized thread tension becomes crucial, but once mastered, the results are garments that move fluidly with the body.

Other advanced synthetics offer specialized benefits. Some thermal-regulating fabrics are engineered to reflect body heat in cold weather while maintaining ventilation. These materials, often used in outdoor gear, are marvels of textile science. For the sewist, they present opportunities to create garments that extend comfort into extreme conditions. Handling them can be tricky because of laminated layers or coatings, but with the right needles and careful seam finishing, they can yield professional-quality results.

Texture and weight considerations further shape the sewing experience with synthetics. Micro-fleece, for instance, is soft, insulating, and lightweight, making it ideal for jackets, blankets, and cozy loungewear. However, its loft can obscure seam lines and cause fabric layers to shift during sewing. Techniques like using a walking foot or basting layers in place can help maintain control. Ripstop nylon, developed originally for military use, has a crosshatch weave that resists tearing. Its lightweight yet durable nature makes it perfect for outdoor projects like tents, bags, or raincoats. Sewing with ripstop demands precision, as the slippery surface resists pins and easily shifts. Clips, tape, or careful handling prevent distortions. Vinyl and pleather present yet another set of challenges. Their impermeability and thickness mean that traditional pins leave permanent holes, and the sticky surface can drag under a standard presser foot. Specialized feet, such as Teflon-coated or roller feet, allow smooth movement, and clips or weights replace pins. Mastering these techniques allows sewists to confidently handle materials that mimic leather without the cost or ethical concerns of animal products.

Blended fabrics combine the strengths of multiple fibers, and understanding their properties unlocks additional versatility.

Cotton-polyester blends are among the most common, merging cotton's comfort with polyester's durability and wrinkle resistance. These blends reduce shrinkage and add strength, making them practical for everyday garments. Spandex percentages play a subtle but critical role in fabric performance. A two percent inclusion might add just enough stretch to a pair of jeans for comfort, while a higher percentage creates leggings capable of significant extension. Learning to read fabric labels and recognize how fiber content influences stretch and recovery helps you select the right material for each project. Tri-blends, often combining cotton, polyester, and rayon, balance softness, durability, and drape. These fabrics are beloved in casual wear for their comfort and appearance but require awareness during sewing, as the mix of fibers may behave unpredictably.

Synthetic fabrics demand technical adjustments, but once mastered, they reward the sewist with garments that withstand wear, adapt to diverse uses, and sometimes even outperform natural fibers. They expand the creative toolkit, allowing projects that would be impossible with cotton or wool alone. The key lies in approaching them with respect for their engineered qualities, experimenting with appropriate techniques, and embracing the new possibilities they offer.

2.3 Advanced Fabric Selection Strategies

Mastery of sewing does not end with handling fabric at the machine. It begins even earlier, at the stage of selection. Walking into a fabric store, or browsing online catalogs, can feel exhilarating yet overwhelming. Rows of bolts, each with unique weights, textures, and colors, invite endless possibilities. Choosing wisely ensures that your time and effort translate into garments that not only look beautiful but also perform well in daily life. Developing advanced strategies for fabric selection is as much about analysis and foresight as it is about creative vision.

One essential approach is matching fabric to the specific requirements of the project. Every design has inherent needs in terms of drape, durability, and care. A flowing maxi dress demands a fabric that moves gracefully, such as rayon or silk, while a tailored blazer requires a material with body and structure, like wool suiting. Similarly, children's play clothes benefit from sturdy fabrics like denim or twill that can endure rough wear and frequent washing. A lifestyle perspective also matters. If you are creating garments for everyday wear, choosing fabrics that align with your care preferences—machine washable versus dry clean only—will determine how practical the piece is in the long run. The most elegant silk blouse may not serve you well if your routine leaves little time for delicate laundering. By aligning drape, durability, and maintenance with the intended purpose, you create pieces that seamlessly integrate into your life.

Quality assessment is another skill that elevates fabric selection. Thread count, often associated with bed linens, plays a role in garment fabrics as well. A higher thread count typically indicates a tighter weave, which contributes to durability and smoothness. Examining the weave integrity—holding fabric up to light to check for consistency and tightness—can reveal whether it will withstand wear. Testing for colorfastness by dampening a corner with water and pressing it against a white cloth provides insight into how the dye may behave during washing. The hand of the fabric, or the way it feels in your fingers, also tells a story. A fabric that feels brittle or rough may not soften with laundering, while one that feels too flimsy may lack longevity. These simple evaluations prevent disappointment and ensure that your effort translates into garments with enduring appeal.

Budget-conscious sourcing adds another dimension to advanced selection. Quality fabrics can be expensive, but resourceful sewists find ways to balance cost with value. Estate sales and thrift shops sometimes yield vintage textiles of remarkable quality at modest prices. Wholesale markets offer bulk discounts, making them ideal for staple fabrics you plan to use repeatedly. Fabric swaps, whether organized locally or online, create opportunities to exchange unused materials with other makers, turning surplus into treasure. End-of-bolt clearances provide smaller cuts at reduced prices, perfect for accessories or smaller projects. By exploring these avenues, you expand your access to fabrics without straining your budget, and you cultivate a sustainable approach by giving new life to materials that might otherwise go unused.

Advanced fabric selection also means trusting your instincts while balancing them with knowledge. Sometimes a fabric simply "calls" to you with its color or texture. The key is to pause and ask practical questions: does this fabric match the needs of the project? Will I enjoy sewing with it? Will the finished garment serve me or someone else in the way I imagine? Combining inspiration with informed analysis ensures that your choices honor both creativity and functionality.

In time, the process of fabric selection becomes second nature. You will feel linen's crispness and immediately imagine summer garments, sense the resilience of ripstop nylon and think of outdoor gear, or run your fingers across silk and envision evening wear. This intuitive connection, grounded in knowledge and experience, is one of the hallmarks of a seasoned sewist. It transforms fabric shopping from guesswork into artistry, allowing you to choose with confidence and intention.

Chapter 3: The Strategic Sewing Space

Studies show that organized creative spaces can increase productivity by up to 76% and reduce project completion time by an average of 23 minutes per session.

3.1 Ergonomic Workspace Design

Before a single stitch is sewn, the space in which you create profoundly influences the outcome. A well-designed sewing environment is not merely a matter of neatness or aesthetic appeal. It is about ensuring that your body, mind, and materials work together seamlessly. Sewing involves long hours of focus, repetitive motions, and precision. Without careful attention to ergonomics, it is easy to fall into habits that strain muscles, dim concentration, and ultimately erode enjoyment. Designing an ergonomic workspace is therefore less about luxury and more about necessity. It transforms sewing from a physically taxing effort into a sustainable, comfortable practice that nurtures both creativity and health.

Height and positioning are the most immediate considerations. The surface where you cut fabric must match your body's natural dimensions. If the table is too low, you bend at the waist, straining your back. Too high, and your shoulders rise uncomfortably, leading to tension that builds over time. A simple rule of thumb is that your cutting surface should align with your hip bone or just slightly above it. At this level, you can lean forward slightly, apply pressure with scissors or rotary cutters, and still maintain an upright spine. A dedicated cutting table adjustable in height is ideal, but even a sturdy dining table can be modified with risers to reach the correct level. This small adjustment has an outsized impact on how long you can work without discomfort.

Seating is equally critical. Many beginners underestimate how much time they will spend at their machines, seated and focused. An ergonomic chair with proper lumbar support helps maintain the natural curve of your spine, preventing the rounded posture that often causes back pain. Ideally, the chair should allow both feet to rest flat on the ground, with knees at a ninety-degree angle. Armrests, while optional, can reduce strain in the shoulders during long sessions of pinning or hand sewing. The relationship between chair and sewing machine is delicate: the needle plate should sit slightly below your elbows when your arms are bent at right angles. This alignment ensures that your wrists remain neutral, reducing fatigue and the risk of repetitive strain injuries.

Tool positioning is another layer of ergonomic design. Reaching repeatedly across the table for scissors, pins, or measuring tapes disrupts workflow and introduces unnecessary strain. Frequently used tools should reside within what ergonomists call the "primary reach zone," the area that your hands can access without moving your elbows away from your torso. Placing items within this arc minimizes movement and maximizes efficiency. Less frequently used tools can be stored in secondary zones, accessible with a stretch or turn but not cluttering the immediate workspace. Over time, developing consistent habits of returning tools to designated spots reduces frustration and creates a rhythm where motion and focus flow together.

Lighting may not seem as tangible as furniture height, yet it has just as dramatic an impact on your sewing experience. Eyestrain is one of the most common complaints among sewists, particularly when working with dark fabrics, fine threads, or intricate stitches. Natural daylight is the gold standard, offering full-spectrum illumination that reveals colors accurately and reduces fatigue. However, not every space has the advantage of large windows or consistent daylight. In those cases, full-spectrum LED bulbs are a worthy investment. Unlike standard bulbs, which often cast yellow or blue tones, full-spectrum lighting mimics daylight, allowing you to match fabrics accurately and notice details that might otherwise be missed.

Task lighting is equally important. A general overhead light provides ambient illumination, but shadows inevitably fall across your work, especially when your own body blocks the light. A flexible, adjustable lamp positioned near the machine eliminates these shadows and highlights the precise area where you are sewing. For cutting tables, broad, even lighting prevents distortion of patterns or measurements. Some sewists even install under-cabinet lighting along shelving units that hover above their tables, ensuring no corner is left dim. The principle is to create layers of light—ambient for the room, task-specific for detail, and adjustable fixtures for flexibility. When combined, they transform your workspace into a place where your eyes can work for hours without strain.

Storage may seem purely organizational, but it is also an ergonomic concern. A cluttered workspace forces constant bending, reaching, and searching, movements that sap energy and concentration. A thoughtful storage system anticipates both the volume and variety of sewing supplies. Vertical storage makes the most of limited square footage. Wall-mounted pegboards, for instance, keep scissors, rulers, and thread racks in plain view and within easy reach. Shelves above eye level can hold less frequently used equipment or fabric bins, while drawers below waist height can contain heavier items like machines or cutting mats.

Mobile carts are another ingenious solution. They allow you to wheel supplies directly to your station and tuck them away when not in use. This mobility supports both organization and flexibility, enabling you to adapt the space depending on whether you are cutting, sewing, or pressing. Clear labeling ensures that tools and materials are retrieved quickly without rummaging. Labels on thread spools, fabric bins, or even drawers prevent the frustration of misplaced items, conserving both time and mental energy. Over time, you'll find that the efficiency of a well-labeled, logically arranged storage system transforms your relationship with sewing. Instead of searching, you are creating.

The psychological benefits of an ergonomic, well-organized workspace cannot be overstated. When your environment supports your body and mind, your focus sharpens. The space itself becomes an ally rather than an obstacle. A clutter-free table signals to your brain that it is time to work. A chair that fits your frame makes long sessions a pleasure rather than a chore. Good lighting invites precision, and orderly storage fosters calm. This harmony between environment and activity is what allows sewing to become a sustainable, joyful practice rather than one marred by discomfort or frustration.

It is worth noting that ergonomic design is not one-size-fits-all. Just as bodies differ, so too will optimal setups. A taller sewist may require higher tables, while someone shorter may need footrests to maintain alignment. Left-handed sewists might rearrange their work zones to favor their dominant hand. The key is to observe your own body as you work. Do your shoulders tighten after an hour? Do your eyes feel tired in the evening? Does your back ache when cutting fabric on the floor? Each of these discomforts is a signal, pointing to adjustments in height, lighting, or arrangement that will improve your space. Listening to your body is the most reliable ergonomic guide.

Creating a strategic sewing space is not about perfection from the outset but about gradual refinement. Begin with the basics: a surface at the right height, a chair that supports, and lighting that illuminates. Then, evolve the space as you notice needs. Add storage solutions when tools pile up, adjust light fixtures when shadows persist, or introduce anti-fatigue mats if you spend hours standing at a cutting table. Over time, these small changes accumulate, transforming your workspace into a personalized studio where both creativity and comfort thrive.

An ergonomic sewing space is ultimately an investment in yourself. It respects your body's limits, protects your health, and nurtures your productivity. More than that, it turns sewing from a physical challenge into a practice of flow, where your hands, eyes, and mind are free to focus on creation. With each adjustment, you set the stage for sewing not as a fleeting hobby but as a craft you can sustain and enjoy for years to come.

3.2 Multi-Purpose Space Solutions

Not everyone has the luxury of a dedicated sewing room. Many people stitch in the corners of apartments, at dining room tables, or in homes that demand constant flexibility of space. The challenge of limited square footage is real, but it can also spark creativity. A strategic approach to multi-purpose spaces allows you to pursue sewing seriously without needing an entire studio. The key is adaptability—furniture, storage, and workflows that bend to your needs and then disappear or transform when daily life resumes.

Convertible furniture is one of the most effective strategies for managing small or shared spaces. A fold-down cutting table, for instance, provides a generous surface when in use but collapses neatly against a wall when not needed. Some models even come with built-in shelving, allowing tools and rulers to be stored in the same footprint. Storage ottomans add another layer of ingenuity. They can serve as seating or footrests while hiding fabric, thread, or small tools inside. Rolling cabinets that double as pressing stations or side tables add mobility and flexibility, letting you wheel your supplies into position and tuck them away once you are done. Investing in multipurpose pieces not only conserves space but also maintains order, reducing the sense that sewing encroaches on every corner of your home.

For those who sew in compact living situations such as apartments or studio flats, the challenge lies in making every inch count. Wall-mounted storage becomes indispensable. Pegboards and hanging systems allow scissors, rulers, and thread racks to live vertically rather than consuming valuable table space. Under-bed storage bins, particularly those with low profiles and wheels, are excellent for keeping fabric stashes accessible yet out of sight. Even ironing or pressing can be adapted with portable stations. Miniature boards that perch on tabletops or foldable full-size boards that slip behind a door ensure pressing remains convenient without permanent sprawl. In such setups, discipline becomes crucial: a habit of returning tools and materials to their assigned homes prevents chaos and allows sewing to coexist peacefully with daily life.

Negotiating shared spaces within households requires a different strategy. If your sewing station occupies a family room or dining area, clarity and boundaries are essential. Clear containers with lids protect projects in progress while making it possible to pack them away quickly when the table is needed for meals. Rolling carts can serve as mobile sewing stations, moving easily between storage closets and work surfaces. Establishing visual order is equally important. Storage solutions that blend with home décor—woven baskets, wooden cabinets, or decorative boxes—disguise the utilitarian nature of supplies and keep the overall aesthetic harmonious. This approach fosters cooperation with family members, showing that the sewing area can integrate seamlessly with the shared environment without creating clutter or disruption.

Flexibility, adaptability, and thoughtful negotiation turn even the smallest or busiest home into a functional sewing environment. The true test of a multi-purpose sewing space is whether it allows you to transition smoothly between creative focus and daily living. When the furniture, storage, and boundaries support this balance, you gain the freedom to sew consistently, no matter the size of your home.

3.3 Advanced Organization Systems

Once the basic structure of your sewing space is in place, the next step is to refine the systems that govern it. Organization in sewing extends far beyond neatness. It is about building a framework that supports productivity, minimizes frustration, and ensures that the energy you bring to your craft translates directly into progress. Advanced organization systems address not only where items live but also how projects flow, how digital tools integrate with physical ones, and how maintenance preserves the life of your tools and space.

Managing projects efficiently requires a system that accounts for their different stages. Many sewists find it helpful to assign specific storage to projects based on where they stand in the process. Bins or folders can contain all the elements for a single garment: fabric, thread, pattern pieces, and notions grouped together. Color-coded labels or tags add clarity, making it instantly obvious which project is ready to cut, which is in mid-construction, and which awaits finishing touches. This approach prevents the common frustration of misplacing a zipper or forgetting which fabric was purchased for a specific pattern. More importantly, it keeps momentum alive, allowing you to pick up a project after days or weeks without wasting time retracing steps.

An inventory tracking system further enhances efficiency. Fabric stashes have a notorious tendency to multiply quietly, leading to forgotten lengths buried at the bottom of bins. By maintaining a simple record—whether on paper or digitally—you gain awareness of what you own and how much. Recording fiber content, width, yardage, and intended use prevents accidental duplication and helps you make informed decisions when inspiration strikes. The same principle applies to notions like buttons, elastic, or zippers. Knowing what you already have curtails unnecessary purchases and ensures that when you sit down to sew, you have everything required at hand.

Digital tools bring another layer of organization. Many apps allow you to catalog fabrics, patterns, and supplies. Scanning fabric swatches and saving them digitally means you can reference your stash when shopping, avoiding mismatched purchases. Cloud-based libraries for patterns not only preserve them against loss but also allow instant access from anywhere. Digital coordination pairs naturally with physical organization. For instance, a drawer of patterns sorted in envelopes can correspond to a digital index, allowing quick searches by garment type or designer. This hybrid approach leverages the accessibility of digital systems without sacrificing the tactile satisfaction of physical materials.

Maintenance and cleaning protocols, though often overlooked, are essential components of an advanced sewing system. Machines require regular care to perform reliably. Lint accumulates invisibly inside bobbin cases and feed dogs, eventually causing skipped stitches or tension issues. Establishing a routine of cleaning and oiling after every few projects prevents problems before they arise. Keeping a small maintenance kit with brushes, screwdrivers, and machine oil near your station ensures that upkeep becomes part of the workflow rather than an afterthought.

Fabric scraps present another organizational challenge. Left unmanaged, they accumulate quickly, filling drawers and bins until they become overwhelming. A deliberate system transforms scraps from clutter into resources. Sorting them by size or fiber content allows for creative reuse—patchwork, appliqué, stuffing, or small accessories. Donating surplus scraps to schools, quilting groups, or recycling programs keeps your space clear while benefiting others. By treating scraps as valuable rather than disposable, you cultivate both order and sustainability.

Cleanup routines complete the cycle. A few minutes spent restoring order at the end of each session saves exponentially more time in the long run. Returning tools to their designated places, sweeping threads from the floor, and covering machines against dust create a reset that welcomes you back to a fresh workspace next time. These rituals also carry psychological benefits. They mark the closure of one creative session and the preparation for the next, instilling a rhythm that supports both focus and relaxation.

Together, these advanced systems create a sewing environment that hums with efficiency. Projects move forward smoothly, supplies remain visible and accessible, and maintenance ensures long-term reliability. The combination of color-coded storage, digital-physical integration, and routine care elevates your workspace from a place where sewing happens to a studio where creativity thrives. The payoff is not only in saved time and reduced frustration but also in a deeper sense of respect for your craft. When your space operates with the precision of an orchestra, each tool and material in its place, the music of sewing flows effortlessly.

Chapter 4: Essential Tools and Equipment Mastery

The difference between a $50 sewing machine and a $500 machine isn't just price—it's precision, durability, and the range of techniques you can master.

4.1 Sewing Machine Deep Dive

Every sewist eventually discovers that the sewing machine is more than just a tool—it is the beating heart of the craft. While needles, thread, and fabric form the foundation of sewing, the machine is the engine that transforms those elements into finished garments, quilts, or home projects with speed and precision. Understanding the features, possibilities, and care of a sewing machine elevates not only your projects but also your confidence. For beginners, the world of machines may seem overwhelming, with endless models, features, and price ranges. Yet with a clear perspective, you can learn to evaluate what matters most, choose wisely, and build a relationship with your machine that supports your growth.

The first distinction to understand is between mechanical and electronic machines. Mechanical machines operate through knobs and dials that control stitch length, width, and tension. They are often durable, straightforward, and less expensive. For a beginner, this simplicity can be reassuring. You learn the fundamentals of stitch formation without being distracted by endless options. Adjustments are manual, giving you direct control over how the fabric feeds and the thread tension behaves. Many long-time sewists swear by the reliability of mechanical machines, particularly when working on basic garments, alterations, or sturdy fabrics.

Electronic or computerized machines, by contrast, introduce technology into the process. With the press of a button, you can access a wide range of stitches, from practical zigzags to decorative motifs. Many models include automatic tension systems, programmable stitch sequences, and built-in memory functions. The benefit here is convenience and precision. Decorative stitches, buttonholes, and specialty functions appear with perfect consistency, something that can be more difficult to achieve on a purely mechanical model. However, this sophistication comes at a higher cost, both in purchase price and in potential repair expenses. Electronic parts are more sensitive to power surges and require specialized service. For some sewists, the trade-off is well worth it, as the features save time and expand creative possibilities. For others, especially those who value durability over variety, mechanical machines remain a preferred choice.

Automatic tension systems illustrate the broader debate between control and convenience. On a computerized machine, sensors adjust tension based on fabric thickness and thread type. This minimizes the trial and error often associated with tension settings and can prevent skipped stitches or puckered seams. Manual control, however, offers an education in fabric behavior. By learning how different materials respond to adjusted tension, you build a deeper understanding of stitch quality. Beginners often benefit from experimenting with both approaches: allowing the machine to handle tension in straightforward projects while practicing manual adjustments when troubleshooting or working with unusual fabrics.

Another major consideration is the buttonhole mechanism. Some machines offer one-step automatic buttonholes, creating consistent results with minimal input. Others use four-step processes, requiring manual repositioning at each stage. Built-in systems offer speed and accuracy, which is invaluable for projects requiring multiple buttonholes, such as shirts or coats. Separate attachments, though slightly slower, provide flexibility and are often included with mechanical machines. Learning to create neat buttonholes—whether automated or manual—teaches patience and precision, and many sewists find that practicing with both methods strengthens their confidence.

Beyond the machine itself, specialty feet and attachments expand what you can accomplish. The presser foot is not a single tool but an entire family of attachments designed for specific tasks. For example, an invisible zipper foot allows you to install zippers so discreetly that the seam appears unbroken, giving garments a professional finish. For beginners, the first attempt at an invisible zipper can feel daunting, but with the right foot, the process becomes approachable and the results stunning. Similarly, the walking foot addresses the challenge of sewing layers or slippery fabrics. It grips the fabric from above while the feed dogs pull from below, ensuring even feeding. This prevents puckering on quilts, stretching on knits, or shifting on silky fabrics. It is one of the most valuable attachments for expanding your repertoire.

Other attachments, such as bias tape makers, streamline otherwise tedious tasks. Creating bias tape by hand requires careful cutting, folding, and pressing. With a bias tape maker, strips of fabric feed through a guide that folds them evenly, ready for pressing and stitching. This efficiency allows you to produce custom trims that match your project, elevating details and finishes. Each of these attachments not only saves time but also introduces new techniques that keep sewing engaging. As you explore them, you learn that the machine is not static but an adaptable partner, capable of evolving with your skills.

Even the most advanced machine, however, cannot perform well without regular maintenance. Lint accumulates invisibly in the bobbin case and feed dogs, particularly when sewing cotton or fleece. Left unchecked, this buildup causes skipped stitches, uneven feeding, and tension problems. Establishing a habit of cleaning after every few projects is essential. Removing the needle plate, brushing away lint, and occasionally vacuuming the area keeps the machine running smoothly. Oil is another vital part of care. Some machines are self-lubricating, but many require a drop or two of sewing machine oil in designated areas. Over-oiling can cause mess, but neglecting lubrication can lead to grinding, stiffness, or premature wear. Always consult your machine's manual, which outlines exact maintenance schedules and points of care.

Tension adjustment is another area where troubleshooting skills become invaluable. Stitches that loop on the underside of fabric often signal incorrect upper tension, while puckered seams can indicate tension that is too tight. Testing stitches on scraps of the same fabric before beginning a project helps identify issues early. Adjusting gradually—turning the dial a small increment at a time—teaches you how your machine responds. This practice demystifies tension, turning it from an intimidating variable into a manageable tool.

Recognizing signs of mechanical wear is equally important. A machine that begins to make unfamiliar noises, skip stitches regularly, or struggle to feed fabric may need professional servicing. Ignoring these signals risks greater damage and more costly repairs. Just as you take a car for regular servicing, a sewing machine benefits from occasional professional attention. Most experts recommend a tune-up once a year for frequent sewists, or every two to three years for occasional use. These checkups ensure that timing, tension, and lubrication remain in harmony.

For beginners, building a relationship with your machine begins with familiarity. Spend time practicing on scraps, exploring different stitches, and learning how each adjustment changes the outcome. Read the manual, not just once but repeatedly as you gain more experience. Manuals often feel overwhelming at first, but with practice, their diagrams and instructions reveal themselves as invaluable guides. In time, the machine will feel less like a mysterious piece of hardware and more like an extension of your own hands.

The sewing machine is a marvel of engineering, combining delicate precision with robust durability. By understanding the differences between mechanical and electronic models, exploring the potential of specialty feet, and committing to regular maintenance, you unlock its full potential. More than that, you learn to trust your machine, to hear its rhythms, and to recognize when it needs adjustment. This partnership between sewist and machine is what makes sewing not just efficient but also deeply satisfying. Each project becomes smoother, each finish more polished, and each session more enjoyable. With knowledge and care, your machine becomes not simply a tool you own but a companion in creativity, capable of accompanying you for years, even decades, of making.

4.2 Cutting and Measuring Precision Tools

Long before fabric meets the sewing machine, success is determined at the cutting table. Precise cutting and accurate measuring form the bedrock of sewing. A beautifully constructed seam cannot disguise fabric that was cut inaccurately, nor can careful topstitching fix a garment that began with misaligned measurements. For this reason, investing in quality cutting and measuring tools, and learning how to use them effectively, is one of the most important steps for any sewist.

Cutting tools deserve special attention because they directly influence both accuracy and the longevity of your materials. Fabric scissors are a fundamental piece of equipment, and not all pairs are created equal. High-quality shears are manufactured with metallurgy designed for strength and sharpness, often forged from stainless steel or carbon steel with carefully honed blades. When used exclusively for fabric, these scissors can last for decades, maintaining clean, crisp cuts that prevent fraying and distortion. Using them for paper, cardboard, or other non-fabric materials dulls the edge and quickly reduces precision. It becomes a rite of passage for sewists to guard their fabric scissors fiercely, often with a gentle warning to household members that these tools are strictly off-limits for everyday cutting.

Rotary cutters add another dimension of precision. With a sharp circular blade, they glide through fabric layers with speed and accuracy, making them particularly useful for quilting or projects requiring perfectly straight edges. Paired with a self-healing cutting mat, rotary cutters reduce hand fatigue and allow for consistent results across multiple layers. For garments, they prove invaluable when cutting slippery fabrics like silk or rayon, which resist traditional scissor handling. The challenge lies in control, as the blade is unforgiving if mishandled, but once mastered, rotary cutters become indispensable for efficiency and precision.

Pattern weights provide an alternative to pins when securing fabric for cutting. While pins puncture the material and sometimes distort the lay of delicate fabrics, weights keep fabric flat and undisturbed. Combined with a rotary cutter, weights enable smooth, accurate cutting that preserves grain alignment. For heavier fabrics like denim or canvas, pins remain useful, but for silks, jerseys, and lightweight cottons, weights often prove the more effective tool. Understanding when to use one method over the other reflects a maturity in sewing practice, as it demonstrates respect for the fabric's particular behavior.

Measuring tools form the second half of this essential duo. The traditional tape measure is perhaps the most recognizable symbol of sewing, flexible enough to wrap around curves and long enough to measure fabric widths. Yet even within this simple tool, quality matters. Fiberglass-reinforced tapes resist stretching, ensuring consistent measurements over time, while clearly marked increments prevent confusion during cutting. More advanced sewists may experiment with laser measuring devices for quick and precise distance calculations, especially when setting up cutting tables or marking long hems.

Specialized rulers extend measurement possibilities even further. Straight rulers in transparent acrylic are essential for marking seam allowances or aligning grainlines. Curved rulers, such as hip curves or armhole curves, make pattern alterations far more accurate, reflecting the natural shapes of the human body. Without them, curves drawn freehand risk unevenness that translates directly into ill-fitting garments. Gauge rulers provide another layer of consistency, particularly in repetitive tasks like marking seam allowances or hems. With a small adjustable slider, they enable you to reproduce exact measurements again and again, ensuring uniformity across multiple seams.

Pattern-making equipment is indispensable for those who wish to move beyond premade patterns. Pattern paper comes in several varieties, from lightweight tracing paper to sturdy kraft rolls. Lightweight papers allow for easy transfer and adjustment, while heavier papers create durable patterns that withstand repeated use. Tracing wheels, equipped with either smooth or serrated edges, transfer markings onto fabric with precision. Pressure control is crucial; too much force tears the paper, while too little leaves faint lines that vanish during construction. French curves, those elegant arcs of transparent plastic, offer professional refinement when adjusting or drafting patterns. They allow you to redraw necklines, armscyes, or hips with smooth, natural transitions rather than jagged approximations.

Cutting and measuring tools might seem secondary compared to the glamour of machines or fabrics, yet they are the quiet architects of every successful project. A garment begins not at the first seam but at the moment fabric is laid flat, secured, marked, and cut with care. Precision here saves countless hours later, sparing you the frustration of seams that don't align or hems that skew. For the dedicated sewist, mastering these tools is not optional—it is the foundation of every creation.

4.3 Pressing and Finishing Equipment

While cutting and measuring establish the framework, pressing and finishing breathe life and polish into a project. Many beginners underestimate the importance of pressing, thinking of it as a chore rather than an integral step in sewing. Yet pressing at every stage—from setting seams to shaping darts—transforms a project from homemade to professional. Just as a sculptor refines form with careful tools, the sewist relies on irons, boards, and finishing machines to achieve sharp edges, smooth surfaces, and garments that hold their shape.

The modern steam iron is a deceptively powerful tool. At first glance, it seems like a household appliance, but in sewing it becomes a specialist's instrument. Steam penetrates fibers, relaxing them so they can be reshaped under pressure. A well-designed iron allows precise temperature control for different fabrics, from the delicate heat tolerance of synthetics to the robust demands of linen. Pressing cloths provide protection, preventing scorch marks or shine on sensitive fabrics. They act as an intermediary layer, allowing heat and steam to pass through without direct contact. Tailor's hams, stuffed into rounded shapes, simulate the curves of the human body, enabling seams and darts to be pressed three-dimensionally. Without such shaping tools, garments risk looking flat and unnatural, while with them, clothing gains the contour and elegance of professional tailoring.

Specialty pressing tools refine these results even further. Sleeve rolls, narrow cylindrical cushions, allow access to tight spaces where standard boards cannot reach. They make pressing sleeve seams or pant legs neat and consistent, preserving shape without creating unwanted creases. Point pressers, often made of hardwood, provide sharp edges for collars, cuffs, or pleats. When fabric is pressed over their narrow surfaces, corners emerge crisp and defined. Clapper boards, heavy wooden blocks, lock in the sharpness of seams and creases by holding heat and steam until they cool. The result is an edge that resists softening and retains its definition even after multiple wears. These tools demonstrate that pressing is not about flattening fabric but about sculpting it into lasting form.

Finishing equipment brings garments to their final level of polish. The serger, or overlock machine, extends far beyond its reputation for preventing fraying. It trims edges, encloses seams, and produces stretch-friendly finishes that standard machines struggle to replicate. For knit garments, it creates durable seams that move with the body. For wovens, it provides clean interiors that rival ready-to-wear clothing. A cover stitch machine, while more specialized, elevates hems on stretch fabrics. It produces the twin parallel rows seen on commercial T-shirts and activewear, offering both stretch and durability. For sewists who aspire to professional results in knits, the cover stitch is invaluable.

Even without these specialized machines, attachments on a standard machine can mimic professional finishes. A blind hem foot, for example, allows hems to be stitched invisibly from the outside, producing elegant results for formal garments or draperies. Mastering this foot requires practice in folding fabric precisely, but once learned, it transforms hems into nearly invisible lines. Each of these finishing techniques reinforces a central truth: the difference between homemade and handmade lies in attention to detail. A garment sewn with care but left unpressed or poorly finished reveals its flaws quickly, while one refined with pressing and professional finishes communicates craftsmanship and pride.

Together, pressing and finishing equipment elevate sewing from a functional activity into an art of precision and polish. They demand patience—pausing to press each seam, testing heat carefully, practicing techniques until they feel natural. Yet this patience is rewarded in every garment that emerges looking not improvised but intentional, not temporary but enduring. The tools themselves are modest in appearance, but their impact is transformative. To press and finish well is to honor the time invested in cutting, measuring, and stitching, ensuring that every project achieves its fullest potential.

Chapter 5: Pattern Reading as a Second Language

Professional seamstresses can "read" a pattern in under 10 minutes, identifying potential fitting issues and construction challenges before cutting the first piece.

5.1 Pattern Symbol Decoding

For many beginners, opening a commercial sewing pattern for the first time feels like staring at a foreign script. The tissue paper sheets are covered with arrows, triangles, dashed lines, dotted curves, and cryptic markings that appear to have no meaning at all. Yet, much like learning a new language, once you understand the symbols, a pattern transforms from an intimidating puzzle into a clear set of instructions. Reading patterns is not about rote memorization; it is about learning to recognize the logic that underpins garment construction. Symbols are the shorthand through which designers communicate with you across time and distance, guiding your scissors and stitches so that your vision aligns with theirs.

One of the most fundamental elements to master is the grain line. Represented by a straight arrow running the length of a pattern piece, the grain line tells you how to align the piece with the fabric's warp and weft threads. This alignment is far from cosmetic. If ignored, a garment can twist, sag, or hang unevenly.

Grain dictates drape, stability, and overall fit. For example, cutting along the straight grain ensures stability in trousers, while cutting on the bias (at a forty-five degree angle) produces fluidity in skirts or dresses. Understanding grain lines is like learning the grammar of the pattern language—without it, nothing else will flow correctly.

Notches are another universal system, marked as small triangles or slashes along the cutting line. Their purpose is alignment. When you join two fabric pieces, notches ensure that curves, seams, or darts match up precisely. Some notches appear singly, others in pairs or even triples, each distinguishing different parts of the garment. A single notch might mark the front of a sleeve, while a double notch identifies the back. Overlooking them can result in twisted sleeves or misaligned seams that compromise the structure of the garment. Experienced sewists often clip the notch inward rather than cutting the outward triangle, reducing bulk in seams, but whichever method you choose, their importance cannot be overstated. They are the punctuation marks of the pattern language, guiding the rhythm of assembly.

Darts, marked by a combination of dots and lines, provide three-dimensional shaping. They transform flat fabric into forms that contour to the body's curves, shaping busts, waists, or hips. On a pattern, darts usually appear as diamond or triangular shapes with dots at the wide end and a point indicating where the stitching should taper. Sewing darts accurately requires precision in marking and stitching, as their symmetry directly affects fit. For beginners, darts can feel intimidating, but once you understand the symbol system—where to fold, where to stitch, and where to stop—they become one of the most satisfying techniques. They demonstrate the alchemy of sewing: how two-dimensional pieces of cloth are sculpted into garments that follow the human form.

Beyond these foundational symbols, decoding cutting lines is essential. Commercial patterns often include multiple sizes nested together, with each size represented by a unique style of line: solid, dashed, dotted, or even color-coded in digital formats. The challenge lies in identifying and following the correct line consistently for your chosen size. Losing track of your size line mid-cut can distort pieces, forcing frustrating corrections. Seam allowance indicators are equally crucial. Some patterns build the seam allowance into the cutting line, while others require you to add it yourself. Misunderstanding this detail leads to garments that run too small or too large. Likewise, fold lines, marked with arrows and often the phrase "place on fold," indicate where the fabric should remain uncut. Cutting these lines inadvertently results in incomplete pattern pieces, forcing you to recut fabric or compromise on design.

Construction sequence indicators form another layer of complexity. While instructions often appear as numbered steps accompanied by diagrams, patterns also embed cues within the layout itself. Symbols may indicate which edges to sew first, where to press seams, or how pieces should align before stitching. For instance, double lines near a seam might indicate topstitching after joining, while small circles often mark gathering points or pleat placements. These details, easy to overlook, determine not just assembly order but also the garment's polish.

Following diagrams requires an attentive eye. They rarely depict every single motion but instead highlight key stages of construction. Recognizing when instructions deviate from what seems logical comes with experience. Sometimes a pattern asks you to attach sleeves before sewing side seams, or to complete a lining step earlier than expected. These deviations exist for good reasons, often to simplify construction or ensure smoother finishes. A beginner's instinct might be to resist, but with time you learn to trust the logic embedded in the instructions. Nevertheless, it is equally important to anticipate potential problem areas. If you recognize that attaching a collar as instructed will trap fabric awkwardly, pausing to reassess can save hours of frustration. In this way, pattern reading is not passive but interactive—a dialogue between the designer's plan and your practical judgment.

One way to build fluency in this symbolic language is to treat each pattern as a text to be studied before cutting fabric. Spread out the pieces, identify grain lines, locate notches, trace dart shapes, and note any unusual symbols. Compare the cutting lines for your size against seam allowance information. Walk through the construction diagrams mentally, imagining how each piece comes together. This mental rehearsal reveals inconsistencies, clarifies sequences, and boosts confidence. It mirrors the way fluent readers can skim a passage and understand its meaning instantly. With practice, you too will develop this fluency, moving from tentative deciphering to confident reading.

The act of decoding patterns also sharpens broader sewing skills. As you internalize symbols, you begin to recognize their impact on fabric choice, drape, and construction. A bias grain line suggests a need for fluid materials, while a cluster of notches around a curved seam hints at potential stretching or easing challenges. Each symbol carries not just technical instruction but also design intent. In this way, pattern reading becomes more than comprehension; it becomes interpretation, a skill that allows you to anticipate results and make informed adjustments.

For beginners, patience is essential. The first few encounters with patterns may feel like slow translation, but progress comes quickly. Each project adds to your vocabulary, and soon, symbols that once seemed indecipherable become second nature. Just as language learners celebrate their first fluent conversation, sewists often recall with pride the moment a pattern "clicked" for them. From that point on, the process feels less like following commands and more like collaborating with the designer to bring a vision into reality.

Pattern reading is not a skill you master once and forget. With each new designer or company, slight variations in symbols and instructions may appear. Independent pattern makers sometimes invent their own shorthand, and vintage patterns often use systems unfamiliar to modern sewists. This variety enriches the learning process, keeping your skills adaptable and sharp. The more patterns you encounter, the more fluent you become in navigating these differences with ease.

Ultimately, learning to decode pattern symbols is one of the great turning points in a sewist's journey. It shifts the experience from dependence on guesswork to independence rooted in understanding. It empowers you to approach projects with foresight, reducing mistakes and building garments that fit and function as intended. Just as fluency in a second language opens doors to new cultures and perspectives, fluency in pattern reading opens doors to endless creative possibilities. You no longer fear the tissue paper sheets but welcome them, knowing that within their markings lies a clear map to transformation.

5.2 Size and Fit Translation

One of the greatest shocks for beginners is discovering that commercial sewing pattern sizes rarely match the ready-to-wear sizes they are used to buying in stores. A person who purchases a size 8 dress in retail clothing may find themselves cutting out a size 12 or even 14 from a sewing pattern, and this discrepancy can feel disheartening if not understood properly. The truth is that pattern sizing follows a different system, one based not on marketing but on body measurements. Translating your unique measurements into the correct pattern size is the first step toward achieving garments that actually fit, and this process requires both accuracy and flexibility.

The journey begins with a tape measure. Bust, waist, and hip measurements form the foundation, but additional dimensions like back length, bicep circumference, or inseam are often equally important. Accuracy here cannot be overstated. Measuring too loosely or too tightly will distort the results and lead to garments that sag or constrict. Standing naturally, without sucking in your stomach or exaggerating posture, ensures that the garment will fit your real body rather than an idealized version. Once measurements are taken, they must be compared to the sizing chart provided by the pattern company. This is where the differences from ready-to-wear become apparent, as pattern companies often build their systems around standardized proportions that do not reflect every body type.

Ease is another essential concept. Ease refers to the extra space built into a garment beyond the body measurement, allowing for comfort and movement. A fitted dress may include only minimal ease, while a loose tunic or coat will include significant allowances. Understanding ease prevents unnecessary worry when your measurements match a smaller size but the garment itself appears larger on the pattern. Ease is not a mistake; it is a design choice. The trick lies in distinguishing between wearing ease, which allows for natural movement, and design ease, which creates intentional volume or silhouette. By studying the pattern envelope and reading fabric recommendations, you learn to anticipate how the garment should feel when worn, ensuring that the size you choose aligns with the intended design.

Many sewists discover that their body measurements do not correspond neatly to a single size. A person may match one size at the bust, another at the waist, and a third at the hips. Multi-size patterns, where several sizes are nested together on the same sheet, make it possible to blend between sizes. This blending requires a steady hand and an eye for proportion. For instance, if your bust measures as a size 10 but your hips as a size 12, you can draw a gentle curve connecting the two size lines, creating a customized pattern line that reflects your unique shape. The key is smooth transitions. Abrupt changes from one size line to another create awkward angles that distort the garment's silhouette. Practicing these transitions teaches you not only technical skills but also a sensitivity to proportion and balance.

Sometimes it makes sense to cut different body areas in different sizes altogether. A person with narrow shoulders but fuller hips may use a smaller size for bodice pieces and a larger one for skirts or pants. The challenge is ensuring that seams and design elements still align. Adjustments must be made carefully so that armholes, darts, and waistlines correspond correctly. This requires both patience and foresight, as even small inconsistencies can lead to garments that twist or pull.

Fit prediction becomes an advanced skill in itself. By studying pattern pieces before cutting, you can often identify potential issues. A bodice that appears too long from shoulder to bust may signal gaping at the neckline. A pant pattern with minimal width at the thigh may indicate tightness in motion. Fabric choice adds another variable, as stretch fabrics naturally provide more forgiveness, while stiff fabrics magnify every measurement discrepancy. Experienced sewists often perform flat pattern measurements, comparing key points on the pattern pieces against their body measurements plus ease allowances. This step reveals whether darts, seams, or lengths align appropriately before a single piece of fabric is cut. In this way, fitting becomes a predictive exercise rather than a reactive one, saving time and frustration.

Translating size and fit is therefore less about conforming to numbers and more about interpreting how those numbers translate into fabric. It requires honesty, precision, and creativity. It invites you to see patterns not as rigid commands but as starting points, adjustable and adaptable to your body and your lifestyle.

5.3 Advanced Pattern Modification

Once you have learned to translate size into fit, the next stage is mastering pattern modification. Patterns are designed for standardized proportions, but real bodies rarely conform to such uniformity. Furthermore, personal style often demands changes to length, width, or design details. Learning to modify patterns empowers you to create garments that are not only well-fitting but also unique reflections of your vision.

Length adjustments are among the most common modifications. Whether shortening a hemline for a petite frame or lengthening a bodice to accommodate a longer torso, these changes must be done thoughtfully to maintain design integrity. Most patterns include designated lengthen or shorten lines, placed strategically where adjustments will least disturb proportions. Cutting at these points and spreading or overlapping the paper preserves the intended shape while altering overall length. For example, lengthening a skirt at its hemline alone may distort flare or symmetry, while adjusting at the designated line maintains balance. When making such changes, it is vital to adjust all related pieces consistently. If you lengthen a bodice front, the corresponding back piece must also be lengthened, or seams will not align. Precision here prevents cascading errors later in construction.

Width modifications present another set of challenges. Adding or reducing width at the side seams may seem straightforward, but such adjustments can ripple across the garment's structure. Expanding the bust area, for instance, affects darts, armholes, and sleeve caps. Reducing waist width alters dart intake and side seam shaping. To maintain integrity, adjustments should be distributed evenly and traced carefully. For those working with multi-piece patterns, changes to one area often necessitate matching adjustments elsewhere. A fuller sleeve requires a corresponding adjustment to the armhole, while a wider pant leg may demand reconsideration of pocket placement. Recognizing these interdependencies is what distinguishes advanced modification from simple resizing.

Style line adaptations introduce a creative element to pattern modification. A neckline can be transformed from crew to Vshape, from scoop to bateau, by redrawing curves while respecting balance points. Sleeves offer similar versatility. A basic set-in sleeve can be reimagined as puffed, flared, or capped, provided the armhole relationship remains intact. Even hem styles invite exploration, from straight to asymmetrical, curved to high-low. Each adaptation requires careful attention to seam allowances, proportions, and structural balance. The goal is to modify design while preserving fit.

One of the most empowering aspects of advanced modification is realizing that patterns are not commandments but guidelines. They represent one designer's interpretation of a garment, but they can be altered to reflect your own interpretation. The ability to redraw, expand, or reshape liberates you from dependence on available styles, enabling you to craft clothing that aligns precisely with your body and taste.

Yet modification is not only about creativity; it is also about consistency. Each alteration must be applied to all affected pieces, and markings such as notches, darts, or grain lines must be adjusted accordingly. Overlooking these details can lead to construction confusion or garments that hang unevenly. Patience is key. Taking the time to trace modifications carefully, test them with muslin mock-ups, and refine them before cutting final fabric ensures that your changes enhance rather than undermine the original design.

As you gain experience, pattern modification becomes second nature. You begin to see every pattern not as a fixed design but as raw material, a template to be adapted. You approach each project with both the technical knowledge to predict how changes will behave and the creative imagination to reshape garments into truly personal creations. In this way, advanced pattern modification represents both mastery and freedom—the technical mastery of proportion and fit, and the creative freedom to design without limitation.

Chapter 6: The Foundation —
Mastering Seams and Seam Finishes

A well-executed French seam is stronger than a serged seam and was the standard in haute couture for over a century—it's still preferred for luxury linens and children's clothing.

6.1 Basic Seam Construction Excellence

Every garment is held together by seams. They are the skeleton beneath the fabric, the architecture that gives shape and structure. Even the most expensive fabric or most innovative design cannot succeed without seams that are accurate, strong, and well-finished. For beginners, seams might seem like a technicality—a matter of joining two pieces with thread—but in reality, they are the foundation of sewing itself. To master seams is to master the very language of garment construction.

The straight seam is where most sewists begin. At first glance, it seems simple: align two fabric edges, sew a straight line, and you are done. Yet the perfection of a straight seam requires a combination of precision, consistency, and patience. The first challenge is seam allowance, the margin of fabric between the stitching line and the raw edge. Commercial patterns typically use standardized allowances, such as five-eighths of an inch, though some modern patterns opt for narrower ones. Maintaining a consistent seam allowance ensures that all pieces of a garment fit together as intended. Even a slight variation compounds across multiple seams, leading to distorted fit or misaligned details.

To achieve this consistency, many sewists rely on seam guides. These can be as simple as markings on the throat plate of the machine or as specialized as magnetic seam guides or adhesive rulers. Beginners often benefit from practicing on fabric scraps, using the edge of the guide to train their hands to feed fabric evenly. In time, the skill becomes instinctive, but during the learning phase, external aids reduce frustration and increase accuracy.

Tension plays another critical role in the quality of straight seams. A seam with uneven tension results in puckering, loose stitches, or thread that loops unattractively on the underside. Testing on scrap fabric before beginning a project allows you to adjust tension appropriately for the fabric's weight and texture. A lightweight cotton voile requires a different balance than a heavy denim, and learning to sense these differences is part of seam mastery. When tension is correct, stitches lie flat and even, creating a seam that looks professional and endures stress without breaking.

Backstitching, though a small action, adds essential durability. At the beginning and end of each seam, sewing backward for a few stitches locks the threads in place, preventing unraveling during wear and laundering. For high-stress areas, such as side seams at the hip or underarm points, reinforcing with backstitching is non-negotiable. Yet balance matters—too much backstitching in delicate fabrics can add bulk or distort the seam. Part of mastering straight seams is knowing when to reinforce strongly and when to apply a lighter hand.

Curved seams introduce a higher level of complexity. Where straight seams rely on consistency, curved seams demand flexibility and control. They appear in countless garment features: armholes, necklines, princess seams, and skirt panels. A concave curve, such as an armhole, requires easing the inner edge without causing distortion. The fabric naturally wants to stretch or gather, so guiding it gently while maintaining a smooth stitching line is crucial. Some sewists find it helpful to stitch slowly, pivoting the fabric frequently, so that the curve follows the machine's rhythm without sharp angles.

Convex curves, like those in collars or sleeve caps, present the opposite challenge. Here, the outer edge tends to push outward, risking a wavy or uneven seam. Sewing these curves successfully requires patience, steady feeding, and careful pressing afterward to smooth the shape. The management of seam allowances becomes particularly important in curved seams. Because the fabric edges must bend, they often bunch or resist lying flat. Techniques such as clipping, notching, and grading address these challenges.

Clipping involves making small snips into the seam allowance of concave curves, allowing the fabric to spread and lie smoothly when turned right side out. Notching, on the other hand, removes small wedges of fabric from convex curves, reducing bulk and preventing the seam from rippling. Grading is the process of trimming seam allowances to different widths, ensuring that when multiple layers lie together, they taper gradually rather than forming a ridge. These practices might seem tedious to a beginner eager to see the garment take shape, but they are essential refinements. Without them, seams buckle or twist, betraying the effort invested in construction.

Corners are yet another test of seam control. They appear in cuffs, collars, waistbands, and pockets, requiring precision to achieve sharp points and clean lines. Sewing into a corner demands accurate pivoting. As the needle approaches the point, stopping at the exact seam allowance distance from the edge ensures that the pivot maintains the garment's intended shape. Lifting the presser foot, turning the fabric ninety degrees, and lowering it again allows the seam to continue in perfect alignment. Rushing this step, or misjudging the stopping point, leads to rounded or distorted corners that undermine the crispness of the design.

Bulk is a common issue in corners, especially where multiple seam allowances converge. Trimming excess fabric, grading layers, or even diagonally clipping the seam allowance across the corner reduces bulk and allows the point to turn neatly. Tools such as point turners or even the blunt end of a knitting needle help coax corners into sharpness without damaging the fabric. Reinforcement is also important. High-stress corners, such as those on pockets or garment openings, benefit from a few extra stitches angled across the point. This distributes stress and prevents tearing during wear.

Pressing remains the silent partner in seam excellence. After sewing, pressing the seam flat before opening it helps meld the stitches into the fabric, setting them securely. Opening the seam with an iron afterward creates a crisp, professional appearance. For curved seams, pressing over tailor's hams or pressing aids preserves shape while smoothing fabric. The discipline of pressing after every seam transforms construction quality, making seams strong, flat, and elegant.

The pursuit of seam perfection is not about avoiding mistakes but about understanding and correcting them. A seam that puckers can be unpicked and resewn with adjusted tension. A curve that distorts can be eased with clipping or steaming. A bulky corner can be reshaped with trimming. These corrections are not failures but part of the learning process, each one deepening your understanding of how fabric behaves and how thread secures it.

As you progress, seams cease to be invisible backbones and become expressions of craftsmanship. They tell the story of care invested, of patience applied, and of mastery earned. A straight seam that runs without deviation, a curve that flows smoothly around the body, a corner that holds its shape—each represents not only technical achievement but also respect for the garment itself. Mastering seams is mastering the fundamentals, and from these fundamentals, every more advanced technique flows.

The beauty of seam construction is that it rewards consistency and attention more than speed. The beginner who takes time to measure, guide, clip, press, and reinforce will achieve results that rival seasoned sewists who rush. In this way, seam work becomes both a discipline and a meditation. It is the slow, steady heartbeat of sewing, the point where fabric, thread, and vision converge into something lasting.

6.2 Professional Seam Finishes

A seam is not truly complete until its raw edges are secured. Left unfinished, fabric edges can fray, unravel, and weaken the structure of the garment over time. Professional seam finishes protect the integrity of clothing while also elevating its aesthetic. They distinguish garments that look handmade from those that appear carefully crafted. Among the most respected finishes are the French seam, the flat-fell seam, and the Hong Kong finish—each with distinct purposes and advantages.

The French seam is often considered the epitome of elegance in finishing. It encloses the raw edges entirely within the seam itself, creating a neat interior that is as beautiful as the outside of the garment. French seams are particularly suited to lightweight and delicate fabrics such as chiffon, voile, or fine cotton, where fraying can quickly compromise durability. They are also favored for children's clothing and luxury linens, where the enclosed edges provide comfort against the skin and longevity through repeated laundering. Executing a French seam requires sewing the fabric pieces wrong sides together first, trimming the seam allowance, pressing, and then stitching again with right sides together to trap the raw edges. While it may feel counterintuitive to begin with wrong sides together, the result is a clean seam that hides its construction entirely. Troubleshooting often involves preventing puckering, which can occur if seam allowances are too wide or fabric is not pressed carefully between steps. With patience, the French seam delivers a result both strong and refined.

The flat-fell seam is another powerhouse finish, known for its durability and decorative effect. It is the seam of choice in denim jeans, workwear, and sportswear, where strength and resilience matter as much as appearance. In this method, one seam allowance is trimmed, folded under the other, and then stitched down, enclosing raw edges while creating a double line of visible topstitching. The finished seam is smooth against the inside of the garment and exceptionally strong. For home goods such as sheets or pillowcases, flat-fell seams withstand frequent laundering while presenting a polished appearance. The challenge lies in managing bulk, especially with thicker fabrics. Careful trimming and precise pressing before the final line of stitching ensure that the seam lies flat rather than creating ridges. Consistency in topstitching is equally important, as the visible lines of stitching draw the eye and contribute to the seam's decorative appeal.

The Hong Kong finish, by contrast, is synonymous with couture refinement. It involves binding raw edges with bias tape, creating a striking contrast or subtle polish depending on the fabric chosen. This finish is especially effective on unlined jackets, skirts, or garments where the inside will be visible. Unlike the French or flat-fell seams, the Hong Kong finish does not hide the raw edge inside folds of fabric but instead dresses it with a narrow binding that both protects and embellishes. The choice of bias tape weight is critical; lightweight fabrics require delicate bindings that do not overpower, while heavier fabrics demand sturdier tapes that withstand wear. Maintaining consistent binding width throughout the garment is a test of precision. A sloppy or uneven binding undermines the very elegance the Hong Kong finish is meant to convey. When executed well, however, it communicates craftsmanship at the highest level, a sign of a sewist who values every detail.

Professional seam finishes transform the interior of a garment from functional to beautiful. They require more time and skill than simple overcasting or serging, but the reward is garments that last longer, feel better, and reflect an elevated level of care. Whether choosing the strength of a flat-fell, the delicacy of a

French seam, or the couture polish of a Hong Kong finish, the sewist communicates pride not only in what is visible but also in what is hidden.

6.3 Specialty Seam Applications

Beyond traditional finishes, specialty seams address the unique demands of fabrics at the extremes—stretch knits, sheer materials, and heavyweights like denim or canvas. Each category presents challenges that test the adaptability of a sewist. The ability to construct seams that respect the fabric's properties is what separates routine craftsmanship from mastery.

Stretch fabrics, common in activewear, dancewear, and everyday casual garments, demand seams that move with the body. A straight stitch, while strong, often breaks under stress because it lacks flexibility. The solution lies in stitches that stretch. Zigzag stitches, for example, create elasticity that accommodates motion. Twin needle techniques mimic the professional cover stitch, producing parallel lines on the outside with a zigzag-like thread path inside that expands with fabric stretch. This not only reinforces strength but also creates hems that resemble ready-to-wear garments. Managing recovery—the fabric's ability to return to shape after stretching—becomes crucial. Too-tight stitching restricts elasticity, while too-loose stitching leads to gaping or uneven seams. Mastering the balance ensures garments fit comfortably while withstanding the rigors of wear.

Sheer fabrics pose a different set of problems. Their transparency reveals every interior detail, making traditional seam finishes inappropriate. Even the neatest overcast edge can show through as bulk or shadow. Techniques such as the French seam excel here, as the enclosed edges remain smooth and discreet. Narrow seams, pressed carefully, blend into the fabric almost invisibly. Handling sheer fabrics during construction is another challenge. Their lightweight nature causes them to shift under the machine, wrinkle easily, or stretch off-grain. Solutions include using fine needles, stabilizing tissue paper beneath seams, and sewing slowly to maintain control. Professional-looking seam intersections require particular care; aligning multiple sheer layers without creating bulk demands accuracy and often hand-finishing. The reward is ethereal garments that float gracefully, with seams so unobtrusive they seem to vanish.

Heavyweight fabrics like denim, canvas, or upholstery textiles bring challenges at the opposite end of the spectrum. Their bulk resists folding, their thickness strains machines, and their stiffness requires careful adaptation. In such cases, seam allowances must be graded, trimming different layers to varying widths so that they taper rather than stack. Flat construction techniques, where seams are pressed and stitched in open configurations, help reduce thickness and distribute bulk. Specialized needles designed for heavy fabrics, paired with strong thread, prevent skipped stitches and breakage. Reinforcement becomes essential in stress points such as pocket corners or waistband joins. Instead of collapsing under weight, well-constructed seams in heavy fabrics enhance durability, giving garments the rugged strength they are designed for.

In each of these specialty applications, the seam is more than a functional necessity—it is a response to the fabric's personality. Stretch fabrics demand elasticity and adaptability, sheer fabrics call for delicacy and discretion, and heavy fabrics require strength and structural management. To master each type is to cultivate respect for the diversity of textiles and to develop the versatility to handle them with confidence.

Together, professional seam finishes and specialty applications form the highest tier of seam mastery. They demonstrate that sewing is not about forcing fabric into submission but about working with its nature. Each finish, each adaptation, tells a story of problem-solving, attention to detail, and pride in workmanship. With every French seam enclosed, every flat-fell topstitched, every stretch seam balanced, and every bulky fabric tamed, the sewist gains not just technical skill but also the quiet confidence of true craftsmanship.

Chapter 7: Closures — Beyond Basic Buttons and Zippers

The invisible zipper was invented in 1958 but didn't become popular until the 1970s—now it's considered the hallmark of professional garment construction.

7.1 Advanced Zipper Installation

Zippers are more than functional fasteners. They are opportunities to combine precision with creativity, transforming garments and accessories with strength, subtlety, or striking design. Many beginners view zippers with apprehension, associating them with broken needles or skewed seams. Yet once the principles are understood, zipper installation becomes one of the most rewarding skills a sewist can master. The zipper is not a one-size-fits-all component; it comes in varieties that each demand unique handling. Invisible zippers, exposed zippers, and specialty applications all represent stages of expertise that elevate construction from competent to professional.

The invisible zipper, true to its name, disappears into the seam when properly installed. The teeth are hidden on the reverse side of the tape, so that only a discreet pull tab remains visible. Mastering this technique requires precision. The first step is preparation: pressing the zipper coils open with a warm iron flattens them slightly, allowing the needle to stitch close enough for concealment. Specialized invisible zipper feet feature grooves that guide the coils, ensuring the stitches run neatly along their edges. Alignment is critical. Each side of the zipper must be attached with identical precision so that when the garment is closed, seam lines match seamlessly across waistbands, darts, or prints. Even a slight misalignment disrupts the illusion of invisibility.

Common challenges with invisible zippers include puckering along the seam or zippers that do not close smoothly. Puckering often stems from stretching the fabric during installation, particularly with lightweight or delicate textiles. Stabilizing the seam with lightweight interfacing or stay tape prevents distortion. Resistance during closure usually indicates stitching too close to the coils. In such cases, unpicking and resewing with a slightly wider allowance restores function. Integrating invisible zippers with lining construction adds another layer of complexity. Here, the lining must be attached so that it conceals the zipper tape without interfering with its movement. Techniques vary depending on garment type, but the principle remains the same: finish the lining neatly while preserving the clean exterior appearance that makes invisible zippers so desirable.

Where the invisible zipper hides, the exposed zipper declares itself boldly. Once considered purely utilitarian, exposed zippers have become prominent design features in both fashion and accessories. Their metal teeth, chunky size, or contrasting colors create striking visual elements that shift the character of a garment from understated to edgy. Installing an exposed zipper involves different considerations than its invisible counterpart. The stitching is intentionally visible, so precision and symmetry are essential. Many sewists topstitch the zipper in place, using decorative thread or contrasting colors to highlight the feature. Choosing the right zipper is equally important: a gold or silver metal zipper conveys sophistication, while a brightly colored nylon coil might add playful energy.

Managing zipper length in exposed applications often requires adjustment. Zippers rarely come in exact sizes for every project, so shortening them becomes a necessary skill. For nylon coil or plastic-tooth zippers, trimming to the correct length and adding a new stop is straightforward. Metal zippers demand more care, requiring the removal of teeth with pliers before stitching a secure stop. This attention ensures that the zipper fits the garment perfectly without protruding awkwardly or bunching fabric. By treating exposed zippers not as afterthoughts but as intentional design choices, sewists can transform closures into focal points that enhance rather than merely secure.

Specialty zipper applications expand possibilities even further, particularly in outerwear, sportswear, and accessories. Separating zippers, familiar in jackets, open completely from top to bottom. Installing them requires reinforcement at the base to prevent strain where the halves join. Proper alignment ensures the garment closes symmetrically, with horizontal seams or patterns meeting precisely across both sides. Two-way zippers, common in coats or travel bags, allow opening from either end. They provide convenience—ventilation from the bottom of a coat while seated, for instance—but add complexity to installation. Each slider must be positioned correctly, and the ends of the zipper must be secured firmly to prevent separation under stress.

In bags, upholstery projects, and protective outerwear, zipper guards or flaps are often incorporated. These fabric extensions cover the zipper from the outside, shielding it from weather or adding durability. In jackets, a zipper guard prevents wind from seeping through, enhancing warmth and comfort. For bags, guards protect zippers from abrasion while contributing to aesthetic polish. Installing guards requires foresight during construction, as they must be integrated seamlessly with seams rather than added as an afterthought. When done correctly, they elevate both function and appearance.

Each type of zipper installation teaches different lessons about fabric behavior, seam construction, and design. Invisible zippers reward meticulous alignment and careful pressing. Exposed zippers encourage bold choices and precise topstitching. Specialty zippers demand structural foresight and adaptability. Together, they represent the evolution of a sewist's confidence, from timid avoidance to deliberate mastery.

The transition from beginner frustration to advanced fluency comes with practice and patience. The first invisible zipper may ripple awkwardly, the first exposed zipper may tilt slightly, and the first jacket zipper may misalign by a fraction. Yet each attempt refines skill. In time, the once-intimidating process becomes routine, and zippers cease to be obstacles. Instead, they become tools of expression and craftsmanship, integral to garments that function beautifully and communicate care in every detail.

Zippers, like seams, are more than technical necessities. They symbolize the union of function and style. A perfectly installed invisible zipper whispers refinement, an exposed zipper announces confidence, and a specialized zipper on a jacket or bag declares versatility. Learning to install each with precision and creativity not only expands your technical repertoire but also deepens your appreciation of how closures transform design. In mastering zippers, you claim a skill that will serve you across every level of sewing, from delicate dresses to rugged outerwear.

7.2 Professional Buttonhole Techniques

Although zippers dominate modern clothing, buttonholes remain timeless. They are seen on shirts, blouses, coats, and even decorative elements on dresses. Their presence immediately communicates craftsmanship, but they also reveal in an instant whether a garment is homemade or professionally executed. A wonky buttonhole, with uneven stitches or inconsistent size, can undo hours of careful construction. Mastering buttonhole techniques is therefore essential, and while machines make the process faster, true artistry comes from understanding both mechanical and hand-worked methods, as well as creative alternatives.

Machine buttonholes are standard in most sewing machines today, and many include both automatic and manual functions. Automatic systems allow you to insert the button into a sensor or foot, which then produces buttonholes of identical length. This ensures consistency across a garment, an invaluable feature when sewing shirts that require a dozen or more buttonholes in perfectly aligned rows. However, these settings still demand adjustment. Buttonhole density—the number of stitches per centimeter—must be matched to fabric type. Dense stitching on heavy denim creates sturdy, long-lasting buttonholes, while lighter stitching on delicate silk prevents puckering and distortion. Without this adjustment, the thread can overwhelm the fabric or fail to hold it securely. Troubleshooting is a normal part of the process. Buttonholes that fray often indicate poor stabilization, solved by using interfacing behind the area. Gaping buttonholes may result from incorrect tension, requiring small tweaks until the stitches lie flat and smooth.

Hand-worked buttonholes occupy a different sphere. Once the standard in tailoring, they are still favored in haute couture and bespoke menswear. Their strength and beauty lie not in speed but in detail. Unlike machine-made buttonholes, which rely on tight zigzag stitches, hand-stitched buttonholes are formed with buttonhole stitch worked carefully around a slit. Traditional keyhole buttonholes, designed with a round opening at one end, accommodate the shank of a button, distributing stress evenly and preventing tearing. Reinforcement techniques such as bar tacks, worked at either end, increase durability in areas of heavy wear like waistbands or coats. Hand-stitched buttonholes are time-intensive, but their artistry sets garments apart. They are particularly valuable in fabrics where machine buttonholes can look heavy or where bespoke craftsmanship is the goal. To the discerning eye, a well-executed hand buttonhole represents refinement at its highest level.

Beyond traditional methods, alternative closures extend the sewist's toolkit. Fabric loops, for instance, provide a soft, flexible alternative to buttonholes, ideal for delicate garments or decorative finishes. They can be made from narrow strips of bias or elastic, stitched into seams or facings. Toggles, often associated with outerwear, provide rustic or playful charm, using loops and buttons of wood or horn. Frog closures, originating in traditional Chinese garments, involve ornamental knotted cords that both fasten and decorate. Hook and eye systems, nearly invisible when installed correctly, are invaluable for securing waistbands, necklines, or areas where a zipper might otherwise gap. Each of these alternatives demonstrates that closures need not be limited to the ordinary. They can become elements of design in their own right, expanding the vocabulary of construction and giving garments distinctive character.

Professional buttonhole mastery, then, is not a single technique but a spectrum. It ranges from optimizing machine buttonholes with proper density and reinforcement, to embracing the meticulous elegance of hand-worked artistry, to incorporating alternative closures that redefine design. Each garment demands a different approach, and the skilled sewist learns to recognize when speed, strength, or artistry should take precedence.

7.3 Creative Closure Solutions

Closures extend beyond buttons and zippers into a wide array of fasteners that balance practicality with innovation. Snaps, Velcro, and magnetic systems each provide unique advantages, and when used thoughtfully, they transform not only the function but also the style of garments and accessories. To treat these closures as second-tier options is to miss their potential; they are modern solutions that can simplify construction while opening doors to creativity.

Snaps remain one of the most versatile alternatives. They appear in children's clothing, outerwear, accessories, and home goods, offering speed and ease of use. The choice of snap type—metal, plastic, sew-on, or press-in—depends on the application. Metal snaps provide durability for coats and denim jackets, while plastic snaps are lightweight and colorful, ideal for baby clothes or craft projects. The key to professional snap installation lies in reinforcement. Snaps concentrate stress on small points of fabric, so interfacing or additional layers are essential to prevent tearing. Placement is another consideration. Misaligned snaps look sloppy and cause garments to sit unevenly, while perfectly aligned ones create crisp, functional finishes. Using proper tools, such as snap setters or pliers, ensures clean installation and avoids the frustration of crushed or loose fasteners. When executed with care, snaps provide a neat, professional alternative to buttons.

Velcro, or hook-and-loop fasteners, entered the sewing world in the mid-20th century and quickly became associated with convenience. While it lacks the refinement of traditional closures, it excels in specific contexts. Children's clothing, adaptive garments for individuals with limited dexterity, and sports accessories benefit from Velcro's simplicity and speed. The challenge lies in using it invisibly. Hook-and-loop tape can appear bulky or industrial if applied carelessly. By stitching it into facings or under flaps, sewists can preserve clean exterior lines while still taking advantage of its practicality. Over time, Velcro does wear, losing grip as lint accumulates in the hooks. Planning for replacement—by stitching tape in accessible ways—ensures the garment maintains longevity. In modern sewing, Velcro's role is not universal but specialized, excelling where functionality outweighs aesthetics.

Magnetic closures add a contemporary, polished option, particularly in accessories. Bags, purses, and clutches benefit from the sleek functionality of magnetic snaps, which close effortlessly with a click. In garments, they appear in coats or vests, offering streamlined alternatives to traditional buttons. However, magnetic systems come with limitations. They are less secure under heavy stress, and their strength must be matched carefully to fabric weight and use. A too-strong magnet can distort lightweight fabrics, while a weak one may fail in thicker textiles. Reinforcement is essential, often with interfacing or stabilizers, to prevent fabric tearing around the snap. Aesthetic consideration is equally important. Magnetic closures can be concealed entirely within lining layers or highlighted with decorative casings, depending on the design intent. When integrated thoughtfully, they elevate projects with modern sophistication.

Together, these creative closure solutions expand the sewist's possibilities. Snaps provide quick functionality with clean lines, Velcro ensures accessibility and adaptability, and magnetic systems deliver contemporary elegance. Each option requires technical care—reinforcement, alignment, and thoughtful integration—but rewards with versatility that buttons and zippers alone cannot achieve. By embracing these fasteners, sewists gain not just practical skills but also the creative freedom to tailor closures to the exact needs and aesthetics of each project.

Closures, in all their forms, are the bridge between design and wearability. They secure garments, shape style, and communicate the maker's attention to detail. To master buttons, zippers, snaps, Velcro, and magnets is to speak the full language of closure, choosing not only for necessity but also for expression. The garments that result carry this mastery in every fastening— strong, functional, and beautiful inside and out.

Chapter 8: Shaping Techniques — Creating Three-Dimensional Form

The average dress form represents measurements from the 1950s—modern fitting requires understanding how contemporary body shapes differ from vintage standards.

8.1 Dart Construction and Manipulation

Darts are the unsung heroes of garment construction. Though often hidden within seams or pressed flat against the fabric, they are responsible for one of sewing's greatest transformations: converting flat cloth into a three-dimensional form that conforms to the human body. Without darts, garments would hang like rectangles, shapeless and unflattering. With them, fabric gains contour, following curves and angles in ways that create elegance and fit. Mastering darts is therefore central to mastering garment shaping.

At its most fundamental, a dart is a wedge of fabric that, when stitched, reduces width and directs fullness. The two stitched lines, called dart legs, meet at a point that releases fullness where shaping is required—such as the bust, waist, or hip. The first step in dart mastery is sewing smooth, professional dart points. Beginners often struggle here, producing dimples or puckers at the dart tip that interrupt the garment's smoothness. The secret lies in tapering the stitching line gradually as it approaches the point. Rather than sewing abruptly to the end, the final stitches should narrow delicately into the fold, sometimes even sewn off the edge of the fabric with long thread tails that are knotted rather than backstitched. This prevents bulk and allows the dart to end in a soft, natural shape rather than a bump.

The relationship between dart legs and length also plays a role. Darts must be long enough to shape without ending too abruptly, yet not so long that they distort the garment. For instance, a bust dart that ends too close to the apex creates an unflattering point, while one that ends too far away leaves the garment baggy. Each type of dart—bust, waist, shoulder, or elbow—has its own proportional guidelines. Observing these relationships and practicing them across different garments builds intuition for how darts sculpt fabric effectively.

Pressing completes the process. A dart stitched neatly can still look bulky or awkward if pressed incorrectly. The direction of pressing depends on the dart's location and the thickness of the fabric. Vertical darts at the waist are usually pressed toward the center front or center back, while bust darts are pressed downward to follow natural contours. Pressing over a tailor's ham, which mimics the body's curves, ensures that darts mold fabric into shape rather than flattening it unnaturally. Mastering pressing techniques is as critical as stitching itself, turning an ordinary dart into a professional feature that disappears into the garment.

Once the basics are secure, the next stage is dart conversion. This technique involves moving the fullness controlled by a dart to a different location while maintaining fit. The principle rests on the concept of dart equivalence: fullness can be rotated around the bust or waist to any position, as long as the same amount of shaping is retained. For example, a side bust dart can be converted into a shoulder dart by pivoting the dart legs through the pattern, redistributing fullness upward. Similarly, waist darts can be transferred into under-bust seams or even into style lines like princess seams.

Converting darts expands creative options dramatically. Instead of being restricted by the placement on a commercial pattern, the sewist gains control over design. A simple bodice pattern can be transformed into countless variations by moving darts into neckline gathers, tucks, or seam panels. Converting darts to seam shaping, such as in princess or empire lines, offers the dual benefit of fit and design. Seams become not only structural but also stylistic, adding elegance or drama while preserving shaping integrity. Understanding how dart manipulation affects drape is crucial here. Moving fullness upward into gathers, for example, creates softness, while transferring it into long vertical seams produces sleek elongation. Each choice has an impact on both aesthetics and movement.

Advanced applications push dart usage beyond the basics. Curved darts, for instance, allow shaping that follows the body more intricately than straight darts. They are particularly useful for garments requiring contour at the bust or hip, where simple straight lines may not suffice. Sewing curved darts requires careful marking and stitching, as deviations show readily on the finished garment. Multiple dart systems add another layer of complexity. Instead of relying on a single dart, two or more smaller darts can distribute shaping more evenly, preventing bulk and creating subtle contours. In tailored garments, you may find both vertical and horizontal darts working together to sculpt fabric precisely to the body.

There are also times when darts themselves are replaced with alternatives that achieve similar results. Ease, for example, distributes fullness across a wider area without visible stitching, often used in sleeve caps or skirts. Gathering, created by drawing fabric into soft folds, provides both shaping and decoration. While less precise than darts, these alternatives suit designs where a softer, more fluid appearance is desired. Recognizing when to use darts, curved shaping, multiple darts, or alternatives like gathers requires both technical understanding and a sense of design intent.

Ultimately, dart mastery is about more than technical accuracy. It is about learning to read the body, interpret the fabric, and apply construction in ways that harmonize both. A dart stitched carelessly stands out as a flaw; a dart executed with precision and pressed thoughtfully vanishes into the garment, its presence felt only in the smoothness of fit. With practice, darts become second nature, their manipulation opening doors to custom design, improved fit, and creative freedom.

Darts, though small, embody the essence of sewing itself: the transformation of flat material into garments that live, move, and breathe on the human form. To master them is to hold in your hands the key to shaping, a skill that bridges craft and artistry.

8.2 Gathering and Easing Techniques

Not all shaping requires the sharp geometry of darts. Sometimes the most effective way to mold fabric is to encourage it into gentle fullness or subtle contour. Gathering, easing, pleating, and folding are all methods that soften construction lines, creating texture, movement, and grace. These techniques not only add beauty but also solve technical challenges, distributing fabric into controlled areas while maintaining balance elsewhere.

Gathering is the simplest yet one of the most versatile techniques. At its core, gathering involves shortening a length of fabric by drawing it into small folds, creating fullness that can be incorporated into a seam or used decoratively. Achieving even gathers without bunching requires attention to both preparation and stitching. Most sewists begin with two or three rows of long basting stitches, placed within the seam allowance. By pulling the bobbin threads simultaneously, fabric gathers along the threads. The key lies in adjusting gathers gradually and distributing them evenly. Simply pulling at random creates bunching, but sliding folds with careful fingers ensures smooth, regular fullness.

Different fabrics respond differently to gathering. Lightweight cottons or voiles gather easily and produce delicate ruffles. Heavier fabrics like denim or wool resist gathering, requiring stronger threads and more patience. Managing fabric weight is critical: forcing thick fabrics into dense gathers results in bulk that ruins drape, while allowing lightweight fabrics to bunch unevenly looks messy. The concept of gathering ratios helps maintain consistency. For instance, a skirt waistband may require fabric to be reduced by half, producing a full, flowing effect, while a sleeve cap may only need a reduction of ten percent for a subtle puff. By calculating ratios beforehand, you ensure that the finished garment aligns with the design intention.

Easing, though related to gathering, serves a different purpose. Rather than producing visible fullness, easing distributes a small amount of extra fabric across a seam so that it fits smoothly into a shorter edge. This is most commonly seen in set-in sleeves, where the sleeve cap has more fabric than the armhole. Without easing, the sleeve would pucker or distort, but with careful easing, it curves naturally around the shoulder. The secret to mastering ease lies in distributing it invisibly. Basting stitches help, but equally important is handling: holding the shorter edge taut while guiding the longer edge gently encourages fabric to conform without gathers. Pressing afterward, often with steam, helps the fabric relax into shape, completing the illusion that no extra fabric was ever present.

Curved seams also benefit from easing. Necklines, princess seams, and hip curves often require subtle adjustments so that one piece conforms to another. Deciding when to use ease versus darts becomes a matter of judgment. Darts offer precise shaping but leave visible stitching lines, while ease provides a softer, more fluid contour. For flowing dresses or blouses, ease may be preferable. For tailored jackets, darts often serve better. Learning to evaluate which technique best expresses the design vision is a hallmark of advanced sewing.

Pleating and folding systems offer structured alternatives to gathering and easing. Pleats fold fabric back upon itself in organized intervals, creating depth and rhythm. Knife pleats all face one direction, producing sleek lines ideal for skirts or draperies. Box pleats fold toward each other, creating symmetry and volume. Inverted pleats reverse the direction of folds, adding subtlety and structure. Achieving consistent pleat spacing requires meticulous marking, often with chalk, tailor's tacks, or even pleating boards. Once folded, pleats must be secured firmly, either by stitching within the seam allowance or by topstitching partway down for decorative effect. Without this security, pleats drift apart, losing their crispness.

Folds, though similar to pleats, can also function as design details, such as tucks or pintucks. These narrow folds, stitched in place, add both shaping and decoration. They control fabric subtly, creating contour while also embellishing with texture. Whether in the crisp pleats of a school uniform skirt or the delicate pintucks of a blouse yoke, folding systems demonstrate how shaping can also become ornament.

Gathering, easing, and pleating are all about negotiation with fabric. Rather than cutting away excess, you redistribute it, balancing fullness with smoothness, softness with structure. They are as much aesthetic choices as technical solutions, providing tools for garments that move gracefully with the body.

8.3 Advanced Fitting Techniques

Even with careful pattern selection and precise sewing, garments rarely fit perfectly straight off the machine. Human bodies vary endlessly, and even the most standardized patterns cannot account for every proportion. Advanced fitting techniques bridge the gap between design and reality, ensuring garments not only fit but also flatter. This process is as much art as science, demanding both technical knowledge and an eye for harmony.

The principle of fitting as you sew is central. Rather than waiting until the garment is fully assembled, adjustments are best made progressively at key checkpoints. After sewing side seams loosely with long basting stitches, for example, you can try on the garment and evaluate fit before securing permanently. Shoulder seams, darts, and waistlines also serve as natural checkpoints. These pauses allow you to recognize problems early—whether a gaping neckline, a tight hip, or an uneven hem—before they become locked into place. Knowing when to make adjustments mid-construction prevents wasted effort and builds garments that conform naturally to the body.

Alteration integration goes a step further, building adjustability directly into the garment during construction. Waistbands with hidden elastic channels, back seams with extra allowance, or hemlines with generous turn-ups all create tolerance for changes in fit. This is particularly useful in children's clothing, maternity wear, or garments intended for long-term use. Even in finished garments, alteration remains possible. Side seams can be let out or taken in, darts adjusted, and hems shortened or lengthened. Understanding how to modify completed garments effectively gives garments longer lives and provides flexibility for evolving body shapes. This adaptability underscores sewing's unique strength over ready-to-wear: clothing can evolve with the person who wears it.

Body forms and fitting tools enhance accuracy. A dress form, padded or adjustable, allows you to test fit without constant try-ons. By pinning fabric or garments to the form, you can assess drape, check proportions, and adjust darts or seams with clarity. However, standard dress forms represent an average body type that rarely matches an individual precisely. Maximizing their effectiveness often requires customization—adding padding at the bust, hips, or shoulders to mimic personal measurements. Custom fitting tools extend this adaptability further. Sleeve boards, arm forms, or hip pads simulate different body areas, providing precision in complex fittings.

Still, dress forms have limitations. They cannot replicate posture, movement, or asymmetries unique to a living body. Final fittings on the actual wearer remain essential, especially for tailored garments. For sewists without access to a dress form, creative alternatives exist. Adjustable mannequins, homemade duct-tape doubles, or padded hangers offer budget-friendly substitutes. These may lack elegance but provide functional stand-ins for more accurate fittings.

The philosophy underlying advanced fitting is one of dialogue between fabric and body. Patterns provide a starting point, but true fit emerges only when adjustments accommodate individual proportions. A bodice that fits snugly without gaping, trousers that follow natural lines without strain, or a sleeve that moves comfortably without twisting—these results are the fruit of careful, progressive fitting.

In practice, advanced fitting transforms sewing from construction into sculpture. Each seam, dart, or alteration becomes a shaping gesture, refining the garment until it mirrors the wearer's form. The skill lies not only in technical execution but in perception: seeing where fabric pulls or sags, understanding why, and knowing which adjustment resolves it. It is a dialogue of observation, correction, and refinement, culminating in garments that are not only worn but lived in with comfort and pride.

Chapter 9: Advanced Construction Techniques

Couture garments often contain construction techniques that are completely hidden—the average couture jacket has over 40 hours of hand-sewing that never shows.

9.1 Professional Finishing Methods

What distinguishes a garment that looks homemade from one that rivals ready-to-wear or even couture is rarely the fabric choice or the basic stitches. More often, the difference lies in finishing. A professional finish elevates construction from functional to refined, ensuring that garments are comfortable to wear, durable over time, and beautiful both inside and out. Finishing is the art of invisibility and precision, where stitches are hidden, edges are secured, and interior details receive the same care as the visible exterior. To master these methods is to step beyond the beginner stage and claim the authority of craftsmanship.

One of the most significant finishing skills is lining construction. A lining does more than conceal raw seams. It allows a garment to glide over the body, enhances comfort, and protects the fabric from perspiration or wear. Properly installed, a lining gives the inside of a coat, dress, or skirt the same elegance as the outside. The challenge lies in creating smooth attachment without bulk. Linings must be cut with precision, stitched carefully, and eased into the garment so that they move naturally rather than pulling or distorting. Lining ease is particularly important: a lining that matches the garment measurements exactly will restrict movement and strain at stress points. Instead, linings are cut with a slight allowance, often a pleat or fold, to accommodate arm movement, sitting, or bending. This hidden generosity allows garments to remain comfortable throughout daily wear.

Deciding between full and partial linings requires both technical judgment and design intent. Full linings, common in coats and formal dresses, enclose the entire interior, providing warmth, stability, and a luxurious feel. Partial linings, used in jackets or skirts, cover only critical areas such as the upper back, shoulders, or waist, reducing weight and cost while still offering structure where it is most needed. An unlined garment, though lighter, reveals every seam and finish, demanding alternative strategies for polish. Understanding when each lining type is appropriate ensures that the interior supports the design without unnecessary bulk.

Interfacing and stabilization represent another cornerstone of professional finishing. Interfacing provides body and structure to areas that must withstand stress or maintain shape, such as collars, cuffs, waistbands, and button plackets. Choosing the correct interfacing weight is critical. A heavy interfacing applied to delicate silk results in stiffness and distortion, while a lightweight interfacing in a tailored wool jacket leaves lapels floppy and unsupported. Matching interfacing to both fabric and design goal requires experience and a careful eye.

Fusible interfacing, which bonds to fabric with heat and steam, offers convenience and consistency. It creates crisp edges quickly and is widely available in different weights. Yet fusibles are not appropriate for every fabric. Heat-sensitive textiles like velvet, chiffon, or certain synthetics can scorch, melt, or lose texture under pressing. In these cases, sew-in interfacing provides a gentler alternative. Hand or machine stitching attaches layers of lightweight canvas, muslin, or specialty interfacing directly to garment pieces, offering control without compromising fabric integrity. Couture traditions rely heavily on sew-in methods, as they allow shaping through pad-stitching, a technique where small diagonal stitches sculpt roll lines into collars or lapels. While time-intensive, these methods yield garments that hold form naturally, flexing with the body instead of against it.

Stabilization extends beyond interfacing. Stay tape reinforces shoulder seams or necklines to prevent stretching. Underlining, an additional layer of fabric sewn to each piece before construction, provides subtle support and opacity, especially in sheer or delicate textiles. Each method operates invisibly but contributes profoundly to the garment's longevity and appearance. A professional sewist learns to view interfacing and stabilization not as optional extras but as integral architecture— hidden frameworks that ensure garments retain their intended silhouette.

Edge finishing is the final frontier of professional methods. Clean, precise edges define quality, ensuring that garments look as beautiful inside as outside. Facing applications represent the most common technique. Facings are shaped pieces of fabric that mirror garment edges—necklines, armholes, or front openings— and provide stability. When applied correctly, facings lie flat, curve smoothly, and remain hidden inside the garment. Understitching, a row of stitches anchoring the facing to seam allowances, ensures that facings roll inside rather than creeping outward. Without this simple step, facings flip to the surface and betray their presence.

Bias binding offers another edge finish, particularly valuable for unlined garments. Strips cut on the bias grain wrap smoothly around curves, enclosing raw edges in a narrow band. This method adds durability while introducing subtle decorative possibilities. Bias bindings can blend invisibly with the fabric or contrast boldly, turning the interior into a canvas of design. For garments where every edge is visible—such as sleeveless tops or lightweight jackets—bias binding offers both strength and elegance.

The Hong Kong finish represents the pinnacle of edge mastery. Similar to bias binding, it involves encasing seam allowances with narrow strips of fabric, usually cut from lightweight silk or rayon. Unlike simple bindings, Hong Kong finishes are often applied with meticulous precision, maintaining uniform width along the entire seam. They are particularly common in couture or high-end ready-to-wear garments, where unlined interiors must still communicate refinement. The effect is both structural and aesthetic: raw edges are secured against fraying, and the inside of the garment reveals a polished beauty equal to the outside.

These professional finishing methods require time, patience, and discipline. They are not shortcuts but deliberate investments of effort. Yet they repay the investment in every way. A lined jacket slides easily over a blouse without catching. A collar supported with proper interfacing retains its crisp roll for years. A dress with Hong Kong finished seams delights its wearer each time the interior is glimpsed. Finishing is the realm where invisible work produces visible excellence.

For beginners, the temptation may be to skip or simplify these steps in the excitement of completing a project. But advanced sewists understand that the essence of professional construction lies here. Finishing is not an afterthought but an integral part of sewing, a stage where garments transform from stitched fabric into enduring pieces of clothing. It is where quality is secured, both in appearance and in wear. To master lining, interfacing, stabilization, and edge finishing is to step confidently into advanced construction, where every garment communicates not only creativity but also technical authority.

9.2 Set-in Sleeve Perfection

Few aspects of garment construction intimidate beginners as much as sleeves. Among sleeve types, the set-in sleeve remains the most iconic and the most challenging. Unlike raglan or kimono sleeves, which are integrated into the bodice, a set-in sleeve is a separate piece attached to a finished armhole. This separation allows for precise shaping and a tailored look, but it also demands finesse in fitting and installation. When done poorly, set-in sleeves pucker, twist, or restrict movement. When done well, they flow seamlessly from shoulder to wrist, allowing comfort and elegance in equal measure.

Understanding sleeve fitting begins with analyzing the sleeve cap—the rounded top portion that meets the armhole. Sleeve caps are deliberately drafted with more fabric than the armhole circumference, a difference known as cap ease. This extra fabric allows the sleeve to curve over the rounded shape of the shoulder and upper arm. Too little ease results in tightness and restriction, while too much creates unsightly puckers. Achieving balance depends on both the pattern draft and the sewist's handling. Cap ease is usually distributed across the upper portion of the sleeve, avoiding the underarm area where bulk would interfere with comfort. Proper pressing with steam can coax fabric into subtle curvature, ensuring the sleeve conforms smoothly without visible gathers.

The concept of sleeve pitch adds another layer of complexity. Pitch refers to the angle at which the sleeve hangs in relation to the body. Shoulders are not identical across individuals—some slope gently, others are more square—and sleeve pitch must align with this anatomy. A sleeve with incorrect pitch twists during wear, pulling against the armhole seam and distorting drape. Adjusting pitch involves rotating the sleeve slightly forward or backward during installation until it mirrors the wearer's natural arm position. This refinement transforms a garment from serviceable to comfortable, allowing sleeves to move with the body rather than against it.

Sleeve length must also be considered in relation to armhole depth. A shallow armhole combined with a long sleeve can restrict movement, binding when the arm lifts. Conversely, a deep armhole with a short sleeve results in excess fabric that bunches unattractively. Balancing these dimensions ensures both mobility and appearance. Measuring on the body, marking on the pattern, and testing with muslin mock-ups all help fine-tune the relationship between sleeve and armhole.

Installing a set-in sleeve professionally requires both preparation and patience. Basting stitches, often referred to as ease stitching, are sewn along the sleeve cap within the seam allowance. These stitches are then gently drawn to reduce the excess fabric and allow the sleeve to fit into the armhole without gathers. The ease must be distributed evenly, avoiding clusters that create puckers. Pinning or clipping in quadrants—shoulder point, underarm seams, and midpoints—helps maintain balance. Sewing slowly, guiding fabric carefully, and stopping frequently to adjust reduces the risk of unevenness.

Even with careful stitching, sleeves benefit from reinforcement. Underarm seams bear the brunt of stress from movement, and adding a strip of seam tape or a small gusset prevents tearing. Shoulder seams may also be stabilized with stay tape to prevent stretching under the weight of the sleeve. Pressing again plays a decisive role. Steam applied carefully to the sleeve cap relaxes the eased fabric, shaping it smoothly into the armhole. A tailor's ham, with its rounded contour, supports this pressing, ensuring the sleeve curves naturally over the shoulder.

Mastery of set-in sleeves opens the door to endless variations. Adapting basic sleeve patterns allows for stylistic diversity while maintaining technical foundation. Puff sleeves, for instance, exaggerate cap ease deliberately, creating volume and drama. Bell sleeves flare toward the wrist, altering silhouette while retaining set-in construction. Understanding the distinction between set-in and raglan sleeves also broadens knowledge. Raglan sleeves, which extend in one piece to the neckline, reduce the challenge of easing but alter the garment's style, creating a more casual or sporty look. By contrast, set-in sleeves preserve a classic, tailored aesthetic. Learning to modify sleeve caps, adjust fullness, or change length allows sewists to design sleeves that align with both function and fashion.

Set-in sleeve perfection lies at the intersection of analysis, precision, and artistry. Each step—fitting, easing, reinforcement, and pressing—contributes to a whole greater than its parts. The result is a garment that feels natural to wear and looks undeniably professional, a testament to skill that transforms one of sewing's most feared tasks into a hallmark of craftsmanship.

9.3 Couture Construction Secrets

While professional finishing distinguishes skilled sewing, couture construction embodies artistry at its highest level. Couture is not simply about outward glamour; it is about unseen excellence, hours of careful labor that ensure garments last, move beautifully, and embody refinement inside and out. The secrets of couture construction lie in techniques that appear invisible on the finished piece but transform its quality profoundly.

Hand-stitching integration remains one of the defining features of couture. In an age dominated by machines, hand-sewing offers control, subtlety, and precision that no machine can replicate. Catch-stitching, for example, anchors hems invisibly, with threads forming small X-shaped tacks on the inside of a garment. The stitches are flexible, allowing the hem to move naturally while remaining secure. Unlike machine topstitching, which may be visible or rigid, catch-stitching disappears, leaving only smooth drape. Pad stitching, another hallmark, sculpts lapels and collars. Worked by hand with small diagonal stitches through interfacing and fabric, pad stitching molds layers into curves that hold shape permanently. A jacket lapel shaped with pad stitching rolls elegantly rather than collapsing, the difference visible only to the discerning eye but felt by every wearer. These hand techniques require patience, but they elevate garments into the realm of couture.

Construction sequence optimization is another secret often overlooked by beginners who follow pattern instructions mechanically. While commercial patterns offer reliable guidance, couture construction considers efficiency, quality, and design intent beyond rigid order. Sometimes installing linings earlier simplifies later steps. Sometimes basting entire sections together for test fitting before final seams ensures accuracy. Knowing when to deviate from instructions comes only with experience, but the principle is universal: let the garment dictate its own logic. Quality checkpoints become part of this process. At each stage— after darts, after side seams, after sleeve insertion—the garment is examined, pressed, and adjusted before proceeding. This slows progress in the moment but saves time overall, reducing the need for major alterations once construction is complete.

Professional pressing integration completes couture craftsmanship. Pressing is not a single final step but a continuous process interwoven with construction. Every seam, dart, and fold is pressed as it is sewn, setting stitches into the fabric and shaping the garment incrementally. Specialized pressing tools expand possibilities: tailor's hams for curves, sleeve rolls for narrow tubes, clappers for sharp edges. Steam and pressure are applied strategically, coaxing fabric into shape without flattening texture. This attention ensures garments that drape fluidly, seams that remain crisp, and silhouettes that hold their intended form. Pressing is as creative as it is technical, turning fabric into sculpture under heat and pressure.

The essence of couture construction lies in respect—for fabric, for form, and for the wearer. It is respect that drives the decision to hand-stitch rather than machine-sew, to pause for fitting rather than rush to completion, to press meticulously rather than settle for good enough. These secrets are not mystical but practical, rooted in care and time. They transform sewing from craft into art, garments from clothing into heirlooms.

For the aspiring sewist, incorporating even a few couture techniques enriches practice immeasurably. A hand-finished hem, a carefully pad-stitched collar, a thoughtfully planned sequence—each adds quality beyond what is immediately visible. Mastery comes not in shortcuts but in deliberate choices that prioritize excellence at every stage. Couture teaches that what is hidden is as important as what is shown, and that true beauty lies in details so refined they escape notice, yet define the garment's essence.

Chapter 10: Specialty Fabrics and Advanced Techniques

Leather sewing requires needles designed specifically for penetrating hide without tearing—using regular needles can permanently damage expensive leather with incorrect hole patterns.

10.1 Stretch and Knit Fabric Mastery

Among all fabric types, knits and stretch fabrics inspire both fascination and fear. Their softness, comfort, and adaptability make them staples of modern wardrobes—from casual T-shirts to athletic gear and swimwear. Yet their elasticity, while a gift in wearability, complicates construction. Unlike woven fabrics, which maintain stable grainlines and respond predictably to cutting and stitching, knits move, curl, and stretch in ways that challenge even seasoned sewists. To master them is to learn not only new techniques but also a new philosophy of sewing—one that embraces flexibility, patience, and respect for fabric behavior.

Understanding stretch percentage is the first key to success. Stretch fabrics are not uniform; some stretch slightly, others extensively, and each demands different handling. Stretch percentage refers to how far a fabric extends relative to its original length. For example, a fabric that measures ten inches and stretches comfortably to thirteen inches has a thirty percent stretch. This calculation is crucial because patterns for knits are drafted with negative ease—the garment is smaller than the body measurements so that it stretches to fit snugly. Misjudging stretch percentage can result in garments that are either uncomfortably tight or sag loosely without shape. Recovery, the fabric's ability to return to its original dimensions after stretching, is equally important. A fabric with poor recovery may look fine initially but will bag at the elbows, knees, or waist after only a few wears. Selecting patterns designed specifically for stretch fabrics ensures that allowances for stretch and recovery are already considered, preventing fit disasters and wasted effort.

Construction techniques for knits differ significantly from those used on wovens. A standard straight stitch often fails because it does not stretch, leading to popped seams the first time the garment is worn. Instead, stitches must flex with the fabric. The zigzag stitch, adjustable in width and length, is one of the simplest ways to create elasticity. More advanced sewists often rely on sergers, which trim edges and sew flexible seams in one pass. Serged seams not only stretch but also resist fraying and create interiors that mirror ready-to-wear clothing. Learning to control a serger takes time, but for knits it becomes one of the most valuable tools. For those without a serger, a narrow zigzag or stretch stitch on a regular machine can achieve reliable results when paired with appropriate thread and needle choices.

Managing fabric during construction is another skill entirely. Knits have a tendency to stretch out of shape under the presser foot, creating wavy seams. Using a walking foot helps feed fabric evenly from both top and bottom, preventing distortion. Ballpoint or stretch needles are also indispensable. Unlike sharp needles that pierce and potentially break fibers, ballpoint needles slide between loops, preserving elasticity and preventing skipped stitches. Handling fabric gently, avoiding pulling or stretching as it passes through the machine, ensures seams retain their natural resilience. Stabilizers, such as strips of lightweight interfacing or clear elastic, can be added to shoulder seams and necklines to prevent sagging over time. These small reinforcements maintain garment shape while allowing stretch where needed.

Finishing knits requires as much attention as constructing them. Necklines are particularly revealing: a stretched-out collar ruins the appearance of an otherwise well-made shirt. Binding, ribbing, or bands cut from self-fabric offer professional solutions. Ribbing, with its inherent elasticity, provides the cleanest results for casual wear, while self-fabric bands blend seamlessly into the garment for a minimalist finish. The trick lies in cutting the binding slightly shorter than the neckline itself, then stretching it evenly as it is sewn. This ensures the neckline hugs the body without gaping. Using a twin needle creates parallel lines of stitching on the outside and a zigzag-like structure underneath, allowing hems and bindings to stretch with the fabric. This technique produces results nearly indistinguishable from factory-made garments.

Pressing knits requires a gentler touch than pressing wovens. Excessive heat or pressure can flatten texture, distort stretch, or even melt synthetic fibers. A low to medium temperature, combined with steam and a pressing cloth, prevents damage while still setting seams. Pressing should be done by lifting and lowering the iron, not sliding, which risks stretching fabric out of shape. Tailor's hams and sleeve rolls are useful for pressing curved seams without distortion. The philosophy of pressing knits mirrors their construction: firm enough to guide, gentle enough to preserve flexibility.

Working with stretch fabrics ultimately demands adaptability. Unlike rigid wovens, which conform to precise cutting and stitching, knits require allowances for movement at every stage. They reward patience with garments that move with the body, resist wrinkles, and provide unmatched comfort. Once mastered, the skills learned with knits extend into other challenging fabrics, building confidence and versatility.

For beginners, the first attempts with knits may feel discouraging—wavy hems, skipped stitches, stretched-out necklines. Yet every mistake offers insight. Each project builds the muscle memory needed to manage elasticity, balance tension, and stabilize critical areas. Over time, what once seemed unpredictable becomes second nature. A sewist who can cut, sew, and finish a knit garment with professional results possesses a skill set that is both modern and timeless, capable of producing clothing that rivals commercial production while maintaining the individuality only handmade work can offer.

Knits and stretch fabrics are no longer optional in today's wardrobes; they dominate everyday wear. To ignore them is to limit both creativity and practicality. To master them is to embrace the reality of contemporary sewing, where comfort, versatility, and professional finishes go hand in hand. With knowledge of stretch percentages, specialized seams, and thoughtful finishing, the sewist gains the confidence to transform challenging materials into garments that not only fit beautifully but also move gracefully through life.

10.2 Leather and Vinyl Applications

Working with leather and vinyl transports sewing into a different category of craftsmanship. Unlike woven or knit textiles, these materials are not forgiving; a single misplaced needle puncture leaves a permanent hole. Their weight, structure, and unique surface properties demand specialized tools and approaches. At the same time, they offer extraordinary rewards. Few fabrics rival the richness of genuine leather or the versatility of vinyl, and garments or accessories made from them often carry a sense of permanence that lighter fabrics cannot match.

Adapting sewing techniques for leather begins with careful needle and thread selection. Leather needles, sometimes called chisel-point needles, have tips designed to pierce the hide cleanly, slicing rather than pushing through fibers. Using ordinary needles risks tearing, skipped stitches, or even breaking the needle mid-seam. Thread must also be chosen with care. Standard cotton thread frays quickly against the toughness of leather, while polyester or nylon provides the strength required for durability. Heavier topstitching threads emphasize seam lines and add visual weight, often desirable in leather jackets or bags, but they require adjustments to tension and stitch length for smooth performance.

The thickness of leather varies widely. Soft lambskin, for example, behaves very differently from dense cowhide. Thin skins drape gently and can be sewn into garments with relative ease, while thicker hides may require specialized machines designed for heavy-duty work. Understanding these variations ensures realistic project planning. Attempting a structured coat in upholstery-weight leather on a domestic machine often ends in frustration, while the same machine may handle soft suede successfully. Vinyl introduces its own considerations. Though synthetic, it mimics many leather qualities, resisting fraying but presenting bulk and stiffness. Its nonporous surface can stick under a standard presser foot, distorting seams unless adapted tools are used.

Specialized tools and machine adjustments are critical for success. Presser feet designed for leather, such as roller feet or Teflon-coated feet, allow material to glide smoothly without dragging. For topstitching, an edge-stitching foot can provide extra precision, keeping lines perfectly parallel to seam edges. Stitch length should generally be increased when working with leather or vinyl. Short stitches perforate the material too closely, creating tear lines, while longer stitches distribute tension and preserve strength. Preparation techniques also differ. Because pins leave permanent holes, clips or adhesive tapes are used to hold pieces in place during construction. Chalk or removable markers, rather than pins, become essential tools for marking. Careful preparation prevents damage that cannot be undone once stitching begins.

Finishing leather edges requires a different approach than woven fabrics. Since leather does not fray, raw edges can technically remain unfinished, yet professional results demand refinement. Options include turning edges and stitching them down, binding them with strips of lighter leather or fabric, or applying edge paints and sealants for a smooth finish. Decorative topstitching enhances strength while adding stylistic detail, often forming part of the design's character. In vinyl, edges may be folded and heat-pressed before stitching, or bound with fabric to reduce bulk. Regardless of the method, consistency is essential. Uneven edges undermine the luxurious impression that leather and vinyl are meant to convey.

Care extends beyond construction into maintenance. Leather requires conditioning to prevent cracking, especially in dry climates. Natural oils or specialized conditioners restore suppleness and protect against wear. Vinyl, though easier to clean, can crack under excessive stress or degrade with exposure to heat and sunlight. Troubleshooting common problems—such as skipped stitches, adhesive build-up on needles, or seam puckering—becomes part of the process. Cleaning the needle regularly, adjusting stitch settings, and practicing on scraps mitigate most issues. Patience and respect for the material ensure that projects emerge both strong and beautiful.

Leather and vinyl sewing may initially feel like an entirely new discipline, but the principles remain the same: prepare carefully, adapt tools and techniques, and finish with attention to detail. Once mastered, these materials unlock possibilities for jackets, handbags, belts, upholstery, and countless accessories that endure for years. Their permanence makes them intimidating, but also immensely rewarding.

10.3 Sheer and Delicate Fabric Techniques

If leather demands strength and resilience, sheer and delicate fabrics require the opposite: delicacy, control, and gentleness. Fabrics like chiffon, organza, silk georgette, and fine tulle inspire awe with their lightness and beauty but test patience with their slipperiness and fragility. They magnify mistakes, reveal every seam, and resist the blunt-force approach that sturdier fabrics tolerate. To sew them well is to learn restraint, developing a touch that guides without forcing.

Handling delicate materials begins with preparation. Cutting is often the first hurdle, as sheers slide across cutting tables and resist alignment. Using tissue paper or a layer of fine stabilizer beneath the fabric anchors it in place, preventing distortion. Rotary cutters paired with sharp blades often yield cleaner results than scissors, which can shift fabric during cutting. Weights rather than pins secure patterns without leaving holes or dragging fibers out of alignment. Every choice during preparation must respect the fragile nature of the fabric.

During construction, stabilizers continue to prove useful. Strips of tissue paper stitched along with seams can prevent lightweight fabrics from being pulled into the throat plate or stretched unevenly under the presser foot. Once stitching is complete, the paper tears away easily, leaving smooth seams. Gentle seaming techniques are essential. A short stitch length reduces visibility while securing the fragile threads of the fabric. Ballpoint or microtex needles, chosen for their fine points, minimize damage. Even thread choice matters; fine polyester thread blends smoothly and adds strength without bulk.

Finishing seams in sheers requires particular finesse, since every interior detail is visible through the transparent fabric. French seams, stitched first with wrong sides together and then again with right sides together, enclose raw edges completely. This finish appears as a narrow, elegant seam that looks intentional even when seen from the outside. For extremely fine fabrics, a variation known as the rolled French seam reduces bulk further. Narrow hems, achieved with rolled-hem feet or careful manual folding, prevent heavy edges that would distort drape. Pressing, too, must be adapted. High heat can scorch delicate fibers instantly, so low settings, pressing cloths, and light steam are the rule. The iron should be lifted rather than dragged, avoiding distortion and shine.

Construction modifications often make the difference between frustration and success. Standard pattern instructions may assume sturdier fabrics that tolerate frequent handling, but delicate textiles require adjustments. Stay stitching curved edges immediately after cutting prevents distortion. Facings may be replaced with narrow bindings or bias strips to avoid heavy layers showing through. Interfacing, if required, should be lightweight and sheer, so that it supports without adding opacity. Specialized finishing techniques, such as baby hems or bound seams with fine silk, replace heavier methods designed for opaque materials. Every modification acknowledges the fabric's nature, ensuring that the garment remains ethereal and fluid rather than stiff or bulky.

Working with sheers demands patience but offers unmatched rewards. The float of chiffon, the shimmer of organza, the delicacy of tulle—all elevate garments to the realm of elegance. With practice, the frustrations of slippery seams or fragile edges give way to satisfaction in garments that seem almost weightless. The key lies in approaching them with respect, adapting techniques rather than forcing conformity. In learning to handle such delicate materials, sewists refine their touch and expand their mastery, proving that skill is measured not only by what can be constructed strongly but also by what can be guided gently into form.

Conclusion — Your Continuing Sewing Journey

Sewing is often introduced as a skill, but by the time one has stitched their first seams, pressed their first darts, and installed their first closure, it reveals itself as something deeper. It is a journey. Each stage, from learning to read a pattern to experimenting with specialty fabrics, becomes less about mechanical execution and more about discovery—of materials, of technique, and ultimately of oneself. This book has offered the foundations, but the true continuation lies ahead, in the hours you will spend with fabric, thread, and imagination.

One of the most valuable lessons to carry forward is that sewing is never static. It is a living craft, continually evolving with new technologies, materials, and design perspectives. Centuries ago, every stitch was made by hand, garments shaped through patience and repetition. Then came the industrial revolution and the invention of the sewing machine, which transformed both fashion and domestic life. Today, the craft continues to expand through computerized machines, innovative fabrics, and sustainable practices. Your own sewing journey participates in this continuum. The skills you learn today are rooted in tradition, yet they also connect you to a vibrant present where design is global and possibilities are endless.

As you progress, you will notice that sewing changes the way you see clothing and textiles in everyday life. A jacket hanging in a store will no longer be just a jacket—you will recognize the type of seam used, the placement of darts, the grain of the fabric. You will run your fingers over a hem and silently judge whether it was pressed properly. Even garments in your own closet may appear differently now, inviting you to consider how they were made and how you might reimagine them. This shift in perception is part of the continuing journey, a sign that you have begun to think like a maker rather than only a consumer.

The journey also invites experimentation. With each project, confidence grows, and with confidence comes curiosity. You may find yourself asking questions: What if I moved this dart to the shoulder instead of the side? What if I replaced this zipper with a row of snaps? What if I cut this fabric on the bias instead of the straight grain? Sewing thrives on such questions, and the answers come not from theory alone but from practice. Some experiments will fail, producing puckered seams or distorted shapes. Yet even these "failures" are teachers, imparting knowledge that no book or tutorial can replicate. Over time, your mistakes will feel less like setbacks and more like stepping-stones.

Your continuing journey will also be shaped by the community you engage with. Sewing is often practiced in solitude, but it flourishes in connection. Online forums, sewing circles, classes, and guilds provide spaces where knowledge is shared freely. Experienced sewists offer advice, encouragement, and sometimes the tough honesty needed to refine skills. Beginners bring fresh perspectives, asking questions that remind veterans of fundamentals. Participating in this dialogue broadens your horizons. You may discover fabrics you've never encountered, techniques you've never considered, or traditions from cultures beyond your own. The craft of sewing is global, and every exchange enriches the practice.

As you deepen your involvement, you may also recognize sewing's power beyond personal satisfaction. It can become a sustainable act, a form of resistance to disposable fashion. By repairing garments rather than discarding them, you reduce waste. By repurposing old textiles into new creations, you extend their life. By making clothes that fit your body rather than forcing your body into ill-fitting clothes, you challenge harmful standards. Sewing gives you agency in a world where fashion is often dictated by industry rather than individual. This awareness grows with each project, turning sewing into a personal philosophy as much as a craft.

Equally important is the recognition that mastery is not a destination but a process. Even professionals with decades of experience encounter challenges. A fabric stretches unexpectedly, a lining resists cooperation, or a sleeve twists despite careful handling. What separates mastery from frustration is not the absence of difficulty but the presence of resilience. Each challenge becomes an invitation to slow down, reassess, and refine. The mindset of patience cultivated at the sewing machine often extends into life itself, teaching lessons in persistence, adaptability, and humility.

Your sewing journey will almost certainly branch into directions you cannot yet predict. Some find themselves drawn to quilting, where precision and artistry merge into heirloom creations. Others explore costume making, delighting in historical garments or theatrical designs. Some discover passion in tailoring, learning the exacting techniques that give suits their enduring elegance. Others embrace the freedom of draping, sculpting fabric directly on a form to invent shapes unconstrained by patterns. Each path is valid, each enriches the craft, and none excludes another. The breadth of sewing is such that you can wander freely, following your curiosity wherever it leads.

Technology will also shape your future experiences. Computerized embroidery machines allow for intricate designs executed with flawless precision. Digital pattern drafting software makes it possible to customize patterns instantly for different body measurements. Online resources provide a wealth of tutorials, masterclasses, and inspiration accessible from anywhere in the world. These innovations do not replace traditional skills but build upon them, expanding the range of what is possible. The needle, the thread, and the seam remain the foundation, but technology extends the walls of the house you are building.

Perhaps the most rewarding part of the sewing journey is the sense of legacy it carries. Sewing connects you to those who came before—grandparents, parents, artisans, and countless anonymous makers whose stitches built clothing long before factories and brands existed. Each seam you sew joins that lineage, a continuation of human ingenuity and care. And if you pass your skills to others, whether through teaching, gifting handmade garments, or simply inspiring curiosity, you become part of that chain of knowledge. Sewing, in this sense, is not only personal but communal, linking generations through thread.

As you move forward, allow yourself both structure and freedom. Set goals—perhaps mastering a new type of seam, completing a complex garment, or tackling a challenging fabric—but also leave room for play. Sewing, at its heart, is creative expression. It thrives when approached with curiosity rather than rigid obligation. A playful project, whether a whimsical accessory or an experiment in color, refreshes the spirit and keeps enthusiasm alive. Balance ambition with joy, and the craft will remain a lifelong companion rather than a burden.

In closing, remember that your sewing journey is uniquely yours. The path laid out in this book provides foundations, but no two sewists will interpret them the same way. Some will pursue perfection in tailoring, others will revel in the spontaneity of draping, and still others will find satisfaction in simple repairs that extend the life of clothing. Each choice is valid. What matters is that you continue to learn, to experiment, and to stitch with intention.

Every seam you sew adds to your story. Every garment, successful or imperfect, reflects not only technical skill but also patience, resilience, and creativity. Sewing, after all, is not just about clothing—it is about transformation. It transforms fabric into form, intention into reality, and makers into storytellers. As you continue your sewing journey, may each stitch remind you of where you've been, guide you toward where you're going, and affirm that the act of making is itself an enduring joy.

www.ingramcontent.com/pod-product-compliance
Lightning Source LLC
Chambersburg PA
CBHW071139090426
42736CB00012B/2168

* 9 7 9 8 8 9 8 6 0 6 9 7 8 *